PRACTICAL ALCHEMY
Path to High Alchemical Arts

AETHYRIUS

TRANSCENDENCE PRESS

To the Higher Genii

Table of Contents

Introduction

At the time of this writing, it has now been 25 years since I was first shown <u>real</u> magic. I was most fortunate that my first teacher in the Hermetic Arts was a true adept capable of demonstrating the phenomenal power of magic. That first time seeing real magic was the singular defining moment of my spiritual life, indeed of my entire life.

In guiding my life experiences toward my purpose, my Higher Genius has seen fit that I study under not just one adept, but four of them over the last 25 years, though they were each very different. There were usually many years between direct studies with them where I was on my own to continue seeking, yet each gave me such significant gifts of tremendous value during my journey that I cannot imagine how my life would be now without their generous instruction.

While it is true that we will always be students on some level while spiritually seeking, there will always be others further ahead on the trail than we are. Those who teach what they have learned continue to have more doors opened to them. It is part of the natural cycle. In 2015, as I near my 44th year it is time now for me to pay it forward to others, those truly seeking and ready to receive just as I was all those years ago.

Though I have not yet mastered the same exact skills as my teachers, I see the path in front of me and I have been shown where it leads. I have had many benchmark experiences that occurred as signposts along the pathway that were required for the journey my Higher Genius has set for me. I have often shared my experiences openly with others in the past, yet more often than not I have resisted 'teaching' in openly public venues.

Although I have always known I would teach 'someday' I was always aware that I was still missing a few key pieces. Even at the urging of others to teach I resisted because it is a real pet peeve of mine that there are too many people who do not possess complete depth of knowledge out teaching in the world, and I was determined not to become my own pet peeve. I am very human, not even close to perfect, and among my finer attributes there are a few personality traits that are less than optimal, but being a hypocrite is not among them. I will not speak from a place that is not my own.

So, now it is my turn, as one in the role of teacher, to give some of those pieces I now understand to others to speed them on their journeys. In wanting to fulfill my spiritual obligations, in alignment with my purpose, I arrived at three key questions:

• How can I do for seekers what my teachers did for me?
• If I were in the students' shoes now, what would be the most helpful things to know in order to make sure they start off on the right track?
• What book would save students much time and unnecessary suffering, and significantly accelerate their progress moving forward?

Having never been an author, I have heard it said that authors should write the book they want to read. I have written a book I would have like to have read near the beginning of my journey. Though it is concise, it covers major key points of distinction most often unknown. The distilled knowledge it contains flows through me now the same as my own blood, and hopefully in time it will for many others.

I have started the series **Illumination Through the Western Mysteries**™ with a book on alchemy because it is the Hermetic Mother Art. Understanding it opens many doors, even if one is more magically inclined, while not understanding it ensures many doors remain closed and locked.

The seeker's dilemma, as it has always been, is knowing how to separate the false from the true. Though this book is not full of typical recipes and 'how to' instructions, it covers important distinctions within basic to advanced concepts while focusing only on what is useful and productive to understand before one sets out on the journey of learning practical laboratory alchemy. It separates the wheat from the chaff in terms of plant alchemy, the first work, so that most of what is currently taught as modern plant alchemy at-large can be happily bypassed as generally nonproductive busywork.

This book is for those interested in an overview of learning about what real practical alchemy is, with a basic introduction to concepts of potential applications as a spiritual path. As the ancient, quintessential, divine mother science, it is not something in which many people have received proper or effective detailed instruction.

Real alchemy, as an ancient Hermetic art, works as a kind of lock and key, which opens the doors to confecting true quintessences for use in spiritual growth as well as elucidating many aspects of deeper and more effective magical practices than many of those currently taught in popular circles today. As the first work in this series, *Practical Alchemy: Path to High Alchemical Arts* lays solid groundwork to approach the subject productively, reveals a deeper path of practical understanding in advanced plant alchemy, and directs seekers toward deeper levels of knowledge in the realms of practical alchemy and magic.

I am not out to convince anyone of anything. My only objective is to present clear information from a classical alchemical point of view and the high magical arts from the same point of view, because they are interconnected, to those who are seeking a more meaningful and integrated spiritual path than those commonly available.

Though I teach with a glad heart because it is my purpose, I do not engage in debate, argument, or adversarial discussion: Those behaviors are engaged in when one feels the need to convince someone of something they believe. I do not 'believe' in alchemy and magic, I know they are real and I understand their highest purposes; therefore, I present information from that place. Though I do hope for the sake of others' evolution that they come to understand what I present, and make an effort to apply practical understanding towards deeper spiritual evolution; I do not hold an attachment to anyone in particular agreeing with me. Validation for me no longer comes from anything exterior, it comes from my Higher Genius alone.

Dare to Do and See It Through!

Aethyrius

I

Presented from the Viewpoint of Hermetic Philosophy

The information in this book is presented from the viewpoint of classical Hermetic philosophy, as its aspects have been taught to me. There are all kinds of viewpoints about all kinds of words and conceptions that circulate about what alchemy is and what alchemy means to certain people. I am not here to say one is alchemy and one is not. I am here to say that, from the classical Hermetic philosophy point of view, there is a specific definition of alchemy, which is the one used within the context of this book, so that there can be agreement on terms in order to clearly communicate.

If there is no agreement on the meanings of terms, there can be no meaningful discourse, so there will be times when I over-emphasize concepts and working definitions by saying things in multiple ways. I will define important terms as I am using them, as they are used in initiatory teaching the way things were taught to me. That enables the meaning that I give to align with a particular understanding without making anyone else's definitions an issue. If somebody wants to align with the definitions that I give because it allows adoption of a paradigm that is more cohesive, that is one's personal choice.

I will always make clear distinctions between what adepts have said to me, what I have been taught, what I have experienced, and what may just be opinion or speculation based on an educated hypothesis that I have not yet tested. By the time I present an hypothesis, I am pretty sure that it is correct and usually will have gotten confirmation from someone whose opinion I feel is reasonably qualified to give one. I try to be really clear about those things, because I think that is really important. There is a time and place for hypothesis in esoteric work, research, and teaching; however, failure to specify when speaking beyond one's actual direct experience as if it were not speculation (a highly prevalent practice in 'esoteric' publications) is both disingenuous and irresponsible.

II

Conceptions About Alchemy

There are a lot of high-level concepts in alchemy, and the word is used ubiquitously throughout all kinds of spiritual and metaphysical literature; however, a classical Hermetic adept would say that the vast majority of the connotations that are used are not necessarily alchemy proper.

One of the most prevalent concepts is that any kind of transformation is alchemy. Hermetically speaking that is not correct. It does not mean that transformation is diminished. What it means is that, while alchemy is transformation, transformation is not necessarily alchemy. Transformation is great, but when working with key definitions, in order to build a context for understanding something much deeper later, it is really important to clarify exact meanings. If somebody has a truly transformational experience, it does not invalidate it by saying, "that is not alchemy," it is just getting the terminology clear within context so there can be efficient communication.

There are lots of modern conceptions about alchemy, and it is good to talk about those from the beginning. One of the things that happens between the magical community and the alchemical community is that, for a long time, there has been a rift down the middle. Part of my purpose is to mend that rift: I am a bridge. I have had training in both sides not commonly afforded to most of those on either side.

In the classical laboratory alchemy tradition, most are a little more left-brained, and then in the classical magical traditions a lot of times many are more right-brained. They have these funny notions which have come about over a period of time.

Lab alchemists have a tendency of believing that alchemy is just laboratory work only, and that most of the magical stuff is just a bunch of fuzzy woo-woo and not actually real. That is because they have generally had very little magical experience, because they are drawn to the lab work.

On the other side, in a much larger percentage of the population, is the magical community. They have been led through various authors in the past, mostly of the last hundred years, to come to the conclusion that physical laboratory alchemy is not necessarily real, that it is mostly a mental or psychological, internal kind of meditative practice.

Both sides are missing the balance of the other. Each of them has important pieces, but it is a lock-and-key system, like a tumble lock—a tumble lock connected to three-dimensional chess connected to another tumble lock. They are deeply interconnected and an accurate functional understanding of either requires a comprehensive understanding of both.

My view, and the integrated Hermetic view of these things, is a more holistic view. Though all of those ideas have their place, it is knowing where they fit in a template that makes a picture, that then makes sense. The Hermetic arts are both art and science, and that means that they are empirical: They can be measured, and they can be tested. In fact, if one cannot measure and test it, that basically means one does not understand; then one goes back to the drawing board until understanding arises. That is the check and balance that a unified approach to Hermetic studies provides. That is the purpose of a properly integrated approach to the Western Mysteries.

On one hand, alchemy is where understanding is proven, because if there is not correct understanding of how to take something, separate it, purify it, and put it back together again, the operation will not be successful. There is no self-deception. There is no fooling oneself into thinking grandiose things that are not actually true; whereas, on the magical side, that check and balance is not there as much. It is, but it is a lot more intangible. One can only produce direct physical phenomena in the magical tradition much further down the path of mastery than one can in the beginning of alchemy, where with accurate instruction much earlier in the process one can actually create something that is a spiritual substance, a true quintessence.

Because the ability to demonstrate phenomena happens much further down the path, and a lot of magical traditions are also approached from a somewhat religious point of view, it is often considered quite inappropriate to question things. In fact, if one questions too many things one becomes the rogue that gets left out. One gets the same basic responses from priests when young, asking questions that they cannot answer, and they say, "Don't worry about it."

The reason why understanding both magic and alchemy in context of each other is important is because the power is in the overlap. It is in the understanding, the in-between part where true initiatory progress is made, because they are both part of each other. Just studying one in isolation helps get a little bit more of certain aspects down, but without their integration there is a glass ceiling, and it is not very far up. Unless seekers begin to integrate both, they never get past that barrier. It is still possible to have all kinds of experiences, but they will be horizontal; there will be no real vertical expansion.

III

Definition of Alchemy from a Classical Hermetic Point of View

The definition of alchemy presented here is from a classical Hermetic point of view. That classical point of view has to do with the separation of the four philosophical Elements, or the three philosophical Principals, depending on how one looks at the process of separating them, purifying them, and then recombining them to create One thing. That One Thing is not a state of being that is found in nature: It is created by philosophical artifice.

I am not saying that there is zero chance that somewhere out in the world there might be a little pocket of quintessence being formed, because I cannot say that. The universe is a mysterious place. Everything that is happening all around us is alchemy. Every aspect of it is a spagyric (alchemical) mechanism. It is separating, going through purifications, and recombining to create the world around us. Nature is doing what it is supposed to do; but it is such an open system that the subtler, finer parts get dissipated so quickly they cannot generally be seen, or captured.

Therefore, practical laboratory alchemy happens in a closed system where it is possible to see and capture all of those subtle components and learn what is really happening. This is how alchemists studied nature, as they often advised Sons of the Art to do. When they said to study nature, they were not talking about the surface level that anyone can see, or even the deeper levels of the external world that we can access today that were not available earlier in our recorded history. They sought to understand the underlying mechanism of all nature, the One Thing that was created by the One Mind. That mechanism cannot be found without doing practical laboratory alchemy.

The idea of the One Thing is really important. It is, in fact, probably the most important thing to get from having a correct Hermetic mindset. That comes from the *Emerald Tablet of Hermes*:

> *In truth, without deceit, certain and most veritable.*
>
> *That which is Below corresponds to that which is Above, and that which is Above corresponds to that which is Below, to accomplish the Miracles of the One Thing. Just as all things have come from this One Thing, through the meditation of One Mind, so do all created things originate from this One Thing through transformation.*
>
> *Its Father is the Sun, its Mother the Moon. The Wind carries it in its belly. Its Nurse is the Earth. It is the origin of all, the consecration of the universe. Its inherent strength is perfected if it is turned into Earth.*

Separate the Earth from Fire, the subtle from the gross, gently and with great ingenuity. It rises from Earth to Heaven and descends again to Earth, thereby combining within itself the powers of both the Above and the Below.

Thus will you obtain the Glory of the whole universe. All obscurity will be clear to you. This is the greatest force of all powers because it overcomes every subtle thing and penetrates every solid thing.

In this way was the universe created. From this comes many wondrous applications because this is the pattern. Therefore am I called Thrice Greatest Hermes, having all three parts of the Wisdom of the whole universe. Herein I have completely explained the operation of the Sun.

This one brief text has so much in it. It was distilled by a brilliant mind and set down for posterity. There is nothing superfluous in this, and there is nothing left out. The work entails coming to understand it so that it can be applied.

Most of the time, though, without true initiatory alchemical teaching, being taught by an adept or being taught by someone who was taught by an adept, what these things really mean is left to very subjective definition, when there is actually a very specific definition.

Most seekers have heard the axiom, "As Above, So Below." The part that is left out is usually the, "to accomplish the Miracles of the One Thing," which is the rest of that concept. It all comes from the *Emerald Tablet*, but the way things are normally presented, that last part is selectively omitted. The, "As Above, So Below," as a fragmented phrase was made very popular by *The Kybalion*, written by the Three Initiates, which may or may not have been William Walker Atkinson. It is not known for certain, but it is known for sure that he was one who used pseudonyms to publish a lot of the other books that were published by the Yogi Publication Society, many of which contain highly suspect content.

Another thing in the next rubric, when it is talking about the Elements, is that "its *inherent strength is perfected* if it is turned into Earth," so that is an important thing to comprehend. The very next thing it says, "Separate the Earth from Fire." If one does not know how to get the Earth out of Fire, one cannot do what it is talking about. That is a really specific thing, and it is a little tricky, but it is impossible if one does not even know what it means. Correct understanding of this one line becomes a key in identifying which processes truly align with adept teachings and which do not.

Someone must explain what these key rubrics actually mean, and part of what I hope to convey is clarity about that. I have created a page for the *Emerald Tablet* on my website, which has a little more information and the Latin version from which this English version is derived.

I go back to the *Emerald Tablet* a lot because it is a constant reminder about the One Thing. The axiom, "As Above, So Below," comes into play because what is true in the macrocosm is true in a microcosm, and must be true in the microcosm of the One Thing in the alchemist's flask. The highest truth on that one level has to also be somehow replicated, or reflected, on the lower level or it is not truth.

The reason I emphasize that is because physical laboratory alchemy is about making quintessences. There are other levels to Western alchemy, such as inner work which is truly alchemical that leads to profound psychospiritual change. From the viewpoint of making plant quintessences though, most of the modern books on the subject are not really teaching people how to make quintessences, but offer only an advanced form of herbalism.

Even if someone had done all of the preparatory work to create a true quintessence, those are made by having what alchemists call the philosophical Sulphur, the philosophical Mercury, and the philosophical Salt, otherwise known as the three philosophical Principals. Those are obtained by separation, purified, and then put back together again to make One Thing.

Putting them back together again is not just putting them all in a bottle and shaking it up; but that is what most people are making and selling on the market under the name of spagyrics, which has become a common naming convention often applied only to plant work in modern teaching, which is incorrect in and of itself.

I am going to get into the distinctions about all of those different aspects so that someone can really tell whether what somebody is saying is real, is actually real or not. What I am trying to give here are the toolsets and the framework to decide for oneself if what is being presented is real or not, based on rules given by alchemical adepts that are seldom properly explained.

IV

Approaching the Study of Practical Alchemy

Plant alchemy is traditionally what is called the *prima* work, the first work. It is the first work in alchemy for a number of reasons. It is far less dangerous than the mineral work, and it is where one learns the overarching level of the processes, to be used later in the mineral and metallic work.

The processes are the same in advanced levels of the work, but there are some things that must be overcome. In the plant work; however, there is a lot less to overcome because plant salts are far more agreeable for certain things than the salts from metals and minerals.

The *prima* work is where one starts, or at least it should be. The funny thing is that there is very little actually published on the *prima* work over the last thousand years. Compared to texts on the work in other kingdoms, there are relatively few texts on the real work as it is done in the plant kingdom.

Until maybe 200 years ago one of the most published topics in the world was alchemy. It was a huge cottage industry. Pound for pound, one could get more for a book on alchemy than a book on most anything else.

It created a huge influx of 'alchemical information' being pushed out into the European world, and most of it was written by charlatans who were really good at copying already plagiarized ideas, and crafting presentation, to make their books look alchemical.

If a scrivener had a certain amount of paper and leather, and was going to make a book, he could get 50 times more for it than he could a book about something else. I can understand why a lot of them were industrious enough to go about doing it. Some of them were probably not trying to be disingenuous, but many of them were. It led to a whole era of discovery that is what we have inherited in the modern world, because it led to a lot of physical manipulation without understanding the theory behind what real alchemists were looking for and why they were doing it, thus leaving out the Mind component of reality, of which adept alchemists were fully aware.

If one looks at our modern sciences, extolled as inherited from the Greeks and Greek thinking, a lot of the later Greeks in their thought processes were leaving out Mind and became very materialistic: That is part of the schism between alchemy and science. That is why today our hard sciences primarily focus on the physical, the main exception being quantum mechanics which is slowly gaining ground in the scientific mindset.

Further problems within alchemical pursuit arise because many of the older texts are sketchy at best. If one does not have training and really know what is right and what is not, it is almost better to avoid them altogether until enough has been learned to make the distinction. The problem with that is that the modern texts on the subject, with few exceptions, are pretty much just rehashed versions of what Frater Albertus taught.

Frater Albertus (Albert Reidel) was a very cool guy. He was an alchemy teacher that taught within the Rosicrucian order, and he was the one person responsible for most of the alchemical instruction, and the energy put into most of that training in the first place.

At a certain juncture, Lewis Spence, who was head of the Rosicrucian order, decided that they were no longer going to teach alchemy, which is bizarre because Rosicrucianism is supposed to be alchemically-based; but they decided they were not going to teach laboratory alchemy.

Frater Albertus said, "Fine. If the Rosicrucians aren't going to teach alchemy, I'll go teach it myself," and that is what he did. He created Paracelsus College and began a seven-year curriculum for the teaching of alchemy along the lines of the classical, philosophical Elements.

That created a whole set of interesting challenges for him. He understood a lot more about the mineral work because there was a lot more written about it. In the course of his studies and research he had made a lot of progress in the mineral work, but because *prima* work starts with the plant work, what he attempted to do was take that classical mineral work training and apply it to the plant work, and he created a process for what looked like classical Elements and how they would be used in plant work.

That was the early 1970's, so for about the last 45 years, that thought process has colored what pretty much everyone thinks is alchemy done with plants. It has led to a whole string of cascading repercussions of opinions about what alchemy is and whether plant alchemy is actually real alchemy because of the results of what those products do or do not do, because they do not line up with classical results—for good reasons, which is one of the practical focal points of this book.

I have always said, and I will say it again here, that is not to diminish Frater Albertus in any way. Without him, most seekers would not be studying this concept openly. Before he attempted to create alchemical teaching from a classical point of view of the four Elements, alchemy was really, truly, strictly the domain of adepts who kept it to themselves and only let in very few people who they felt were ready and appropriate, and worth their time.

Adepts are a grumpy bunch, for the most part. They do not have to take nonsense, and they do not. They are usually very isolated, and isolation tends to make people a little less sociable. Adepts are no exception to that. They like each other's company and that is about it. Other people do not have anything to say that they feel is worth hearing most of the time, because they live in a paradigm the adept has moved beyond. From a certain point of view, I can understand that, but that does not help those who are still seeking. Furthermore, adept-pupil relationships are by necessity traditionally one-on-one relationships so teaching the masses has never been an adept agenda, nor even a remote concern.

What Frater Albertus did, as I present certain parts of it, even broken as it is, was still an incredible launching point to help masses of seekers move forward. Sometimes one figures out what something is by first figuring out what it is not: Part of what he did was contribute to the discussion of figuring that out, though decades later.

He was a master, by the time he died. Most people are not aware of the fact that he actually created the Philosopher's Stone. Not only could he create it, he could do it in a weekend from scratch, start to finish, and do a transmutation as proof of the Stone. He only did that in front of a few people. He did that in front of a teacher of an alchemist that I know and trust. That is the only reason I know myself.

I do not know if most of the people that are carrying on the legacy of Frater Albertus know that. From the way that they teach and the things that they do, I have the working assumption that they do not, which means that he chose to segment who he showed and who he did not. The people that one would think would have been closest to him, that were around him the most, may not have gotten to see that, because his demonstration was given in New Zealand. He did not do it in the U.S. where he normally taught.

It does make me scratch my head sometimes and wonder why he made those choices, but clearly, as a master, he had a reason. It is not to question it, but it is to know that he did succeed in that work. However, at the beginning of his alchemical trek he was not a master, and the *prima* curriculum that he created was his best attempt at recreating classical alchemy in that kingdom. If he got to do it over again, I would like to think he would have done it differently.

It is important to take all of this and place what is taught in Albertus plant work in juxtaposition to what is clearly stated in the *Emerald Tablet*. It does not line up as neatly as many seem to believe because they continue to teach it the same way. Understanding the distinctions is paramount to moving forward into a more accurate and useful (practical) understanding of alchemy and the Great Work. In order to do that, there is some more ground work to cover.

V

Understanding Alchemy's Place within Hermetic Sciences

The two main branches of Hermetic philosophy are alchemy and magic. There are a lot of other things that are labeled Hermetic, because they flow from those ideas; and because most people have not had access to really true initiatory teaching in alchemy and magic, other Hermetic practices, that are the Lesser Arts, have become very popular.

Divination, esoteric symbolism, astrology—those things all still stem from the same source. They are just substantially distanced from the root, and because of that, have eroded and morphed into concepts and practices that were not part of original instruction. At one point, they were all interconnected in the way that they were taught in the mystery temples within ancient initiatory systems. They were all aspects of one another that were used and taught to reflect each other within a holism, a truly complete thing.

I feel, and it has been said by adepts, that situation was true in Egypt at a certain point of time. Later on, as Egyptian priests became corrupt and Egypt was conquered by the Greeks, the Egyptians never trusted Greeks so they did not teach them the deeper levels of their teachings. After the Greeks became pharaohs it all went downhill.

Fortunately, the pure initiatory stream left Egypt a couple millennia before the Ptolemaic dynasty and went elsewhere, through various mechanisms.[1] That is why it was able to be preserved in other places, albeit in fragmented condition. Traces of it are everywhere if one knows what to look for, it is just that most of the time they are presented through the stilted view of academia and not from a truly initiatory point of view.

That initiatory point of view of alchemy as the mother science of all Hermetic wisdom is of utmost importance because it reveals the mechanics of what makes magic function, regardless of one's tradition. It does not matter whether one is Roman Catholic, Wiccan, Hermetic, Kabbalistic, Rosicrucian, Martinist, or a practitioner of Voodoo. The mechanics of reality are defined by the aspects described in the *Emerald Tablet* and they are the same for everyone whether they choose to recognize it or not. It is just the way the mechanics of reality work.

The mechanics of how it works on each different level of reality is part of what the alchemist has to try to come to understand. The thing about approaching everything from this paradigm as a check and balance system is that, if it is true on one level, it is true on all levels; if it is not true on all levels, it is not true. That

---

[1] This is a vast, long, winding subject that I will be presenting in future work.

is the basic working truth of the axiom "As Above, So Below, to Accomplish the Miracles of the One Thing."

Now, how it is true on each level does not necessarily look the same. What one learns to do in the lab work is a physical mechanical process that has a lot more aspects to it that just the physical manipulation; but it teaches one the mechanics. The entire purpose of that, aside from obtaining quintessence on whatever level one is able to obtain it, is to then understand the mechanism itself, so that it can then begin to be applied to the mind.

The mind is not physical in the sense where one can manipulate it in a lab process, but there is a mechanism that must be understood in order to fully enter that overlap space between alchemy and magic that I mentioned being so important. It is the understanding of the mechanics, and not just the manipulation but the underlying deeper capital 'U' understanding of why certain things are done.

If one understands the theory and the why, eventually one can find the way through it. If one just has a recipe and no real understanding, success in any capacity is unlikely. There is always stuff left out of the recipe, just like a lot of magical practice was based on grimoires that circulated heavily, and most of them were subject to the same plagiarized bastardization as alchemical texts.

If one understands the concept of grimoires, which were practitioners' working notes kept all in one place, one would know that none of them ever wrote everything down. They are like my notes for the lecture from which this book was later created. There are many gaps in those grimoires, even if they are real, simply because of the nature of what they are.

People that do not have any true initiatory training, that do not have any of those spaces filled in, are just running around doing the steps in the grimoire thinking that they understand something. They do not understand anything. They are just trying to replicate what they think is a complete process.

Some of them, if they are studying other things and they have connected a few more dots, will figure a few things out, and then they may have some success with a magical operation. If they actually succeed in any kind of evocation, then they may be able to receive direct instruction from an intelligence that may or may not be trusted; but, at least it is progress of a sort.

The thing that I really like about understanding alchemy's place within the Hermetic sciences is that, if one comes to understand it on a deeper level, its validation can then be seen in other things. Commonalities can be seen clearly.

Amongst all the different magical traditions, they all have their different ideas. The one thing that is universal to all of them is alchemy. They will all agree to that. It is just that there are very few of them that actually have had initiatory training in alchemy to be able to make meaning from that commonality. That is part of what I am driven in the direction of doing: Helping people understand alchemy so that they can actually make more meaning within their own tradition, without ever having to step outside of it.

It does not matter if one is Roman Catholic, a witch, or a Jewish mystic. It does not matter because the mechanics are the same for everyone. All of those traditions have their own deeper initiatory paths. They are all there.

This is why my introductory magic lecture takes four days, because of showing where these aspects are in each system to allow people to see that, just because somebody is led to be more devotional and, therefore, being Roman Catholic is a more fulfilling religious path for them, and somebody else feels more witchy and relates to the universe through a slightly different lens, does not mean at the end of the day that either one of them are doing anything any different. It is just that the way the path winds is more conducive to what each person needs in a particular incarnation. That is all it means.

Being able to see the processes of alchemy, if each in those traditions could do that, the purity of their paths could be restored without ever having to step outside them. If they choose to, because they are led to, that is a whole other thing. Alchemy is a path in and of itself, but it is not exclusionary, except to those who do not understand.

The thing that is really cool about it is that seekers really do learn how to view the different aspects of many things. In plant alchemy one learns how to separate the spirit, soul, and body of the plant, purify them, and put them back together again to create this new One Thing that alchemists call a quintessence, which is a condition of being not found in nature, but which has to be brought about by philosophical art.

What does that mean? It means that the same thing has to be applied on other levels of being, like the mental level, in order to do real inner alchemy work. Grasping this then makes one look at the mechanics of religions, to identify where they have concealed their original understanding of different universal functions within the allegories of their traditions.

If one just wants to be devotional and not do theurgy, god working, then it does not matter; but if what a person really craves is a religious path that is actually bringing them conscious evolution that can be experienced and accelerated in one lifetime, then it really does matter. That is what a lot of modern 'magical' organizations purport to offer but have lost; or they are revivalist traditions that did not lose it, but are still trying to find it.

There is nothing wrong with either of those. All of them have contributed to the overall conversation. Though some contributions, however well-intended, can have undesirable long-term consequences. For instance, there are concepts that the Theosophical Society put out into the world that have become embedded in the mindset of a lot of the magical community that are things that Madame Blavatsky just made up and wrote down because they were her hypotheses at the time.

If she had gotten to live for another hundred years, she would likely have very different hypotheses by now, but people have been dragging her concepts around for a century. She was not a true initiate, she was just a psychic medium with a penchant for intense research, which was really what she excelled at more than anything she ever taught. She did some really awesome research that allowed me to connect a few dots in my own research in places I would likely not have been able to do if it had not been for the research that she compiled. And yet, she is only one of many whose ideas have tainted modern magical thought with turn-of-the-century, Victorian era, concepts that really hinder more than assist in attaining deeper magical understanding.

We all stand on the shoulders of these people that were human, that were doing the best they could, and contributed to the conversation. It is unfair to penalize their memory for doing the best they could in a bygone era with far less access to information than we have today. These were people who literally hiked to Tibet to seek out anything of substance they could find, whereas most of us today just sit down in front of a computer. If those people were still around in the same body, they would know a whole lot more by now, given an extra century to go dig around and search. But, all we ever have are frozen encapsulations, and all we can do is extract from that: Take from it what is useful, and the rest of it is just there. I do not have to judge it, or make it right or wrong. I just do not have to pick it up and carry it around with me.

One of the pinnacles of growing in alchemical understanding is being able to take what can be seen in the constructs that have been created for spiritual growth and break them down, look at them, and see what really lines up with a classical alchemical point of view and where things fall off track. It explains why there are so many kinds of belief systems, like 1,600 denominations of Christianity, all adopting slightly different viewpoints. Inability to embrace deeper underlying commonality causes a continual fracturing until there is little cohesive value left. This is a cycle that persists in all great religions, because over time there are too many aberrations of the original ideas from which they were founded.

Eventually the alchemical process results in a breakdown, a complete and total breakdown of the whole thing, and then something new is created out of it. This is why major religions go through 2,000-year cycles: Within what we have as our recorded history there are 4,000-year and 2,000-year lifespans for most major religions. Some of them overlap, of course, but the lifespan of those religions which start off in a creative way, over time have enough aberrations and elaborations that eventually it all dissolves. Then, by necessity something new comes out of all of that fertilized, dissolved chaos.

Christianity, whether most people want to agree with it or not, was, by the time the Church of Rome got hold of it at least, a recreation of the entire Egyptian religion. It was a theocratic recreation. The reason they got away with nobody figuring that out for nearly 1,600 years was because nobody could accurately translate hieroglyphics until several decades after the Rosetta Stone was found in 1799 on the Napoleonic expedition to Egypt.

They basically, part and parcel, hoodwinked the entire Egyptian religion and repackaged it. That does not invalidate it, because the concepts that were embedded within Egyptian religion were perennial. The same thing within Catholicism: 'catholic' means universal. That was their attempt at catalyzing what they understood of perennial wisdom into a new theocratic power. They were using a slightly different allegory which was pinned to a specific person who had a physical existence, which is one of the clever things about allegory and the way it is used in religion.

Every single aspect of those two religions lines up, down to even the corruptions that happened a thousand years after they were created. It is easy to think that a lot of the things that the priests in the Church of Rome did that were corrupt were innovative and new. They were not new at all. They stole those too, like the selling of indulgences, or absolutions. That was stuff the Egyptians did nearly 1,000 years before the Church of Rome ever even came about. It is easily seen in the changes that occur within the drawings on the walls of the processes that describe how the scales of Ma'at, when a person died, would weigh the heart against a feather. For a long time it was just the scales and the feather, and if the heart were not lighter than a feather then Ammit was there to devour the soul. If it were lighter, then it shows the rest of the process.

At a certain point in time, there develops this change in the way it was being presented where Horus is standing there holding up the end with the heart to make it lighter than the feather. Horus, being the son of Isis and Osiris, the Christos figure in that trinity, is basically lifting the burden of transgressions in order to pass being devoured by Ammit. Thus, the use of vicarious atonement far preceded ideas now claimed as originally Christian.

That story is not new. There were lots and lots of savior gods before this was all pinned on Jesus, but in the Egyptian it can be seen plain as day; the full transition and exactly what they did. That is when the selling of indulgences within the Egyptian religion came about. The priests of Amun became corrupt, which after a while usually happens in any religion that exists for long spans of time. In this case in particular, it happened in Egypt after the heart of the perennial wisdom it once offered had long departed, taking the true pharaonic science with it.

Those same things were happening in the Church of Rome. Martin Luther tried to fix it. His intention was never to not be Catholic. It was never to create a schism. It was never to do any of that. It was just to fix the problems. If he could have become Pope there might not have ever been a schism. Yet, everything has to go through its evolution and eventually eat its own shadow.

There are many things one begins to be able to see when connecting the dots in these processes, that makes the learning of it exciting but also illuminating. Many turn to alternative paths specifically because of the holes in religious dogma that indoctrinates the ignorant, and labels that which could illuminate as 'bad' or 'forbidden.' Of course, those were the first places I wanted to go. Not because I wanted to be rebellious, but because I wanted answers. At a certain point I would have locked horns with the Devil to get answers.

At a certain point in spiritual evolution, one can reach such an apex of divine discontent that one is then willing to empty one's cup of what they think they know, in order for it to be filled by what one's Higher Genius wishes one to drink.

I never did try to talk to the Devil all that time ago, only because it became unnecessary. That is a good thing, as I am certain it would not have been a pleasant experience at that point in my development. Now, however, it would be like, "Oh, it is nice to see you." There would not be fear about it. I understand that role now and its vast importance, because there is a mechanistic need for that universal function (which is also a cunning intelligence), without which we would not be able to exist physically to be here at all, in order to evolve outside of spiritual unity. That Guardian function is of utmost importance, regardless of how maliciously maligned its personifications have been over the last couple millennia.[2]

---

[2] The Guardian is a very complex topic that will be covered in a future work on initiatory magic, as it is too far outside the focus of this overview.

VI

Schism Between Alchemy & Magic

Alchemy and magic were both considered complementary aspects of the same divine science, being Hermetic arts.

Alchemy has more often been used in reference to physical substances, and magic more the manipulation of mental forces, but both of them always within the context that all was Mind. Later though, there were many in the alchemical laboratory tradition that really did not get the deeper concept and who were just trying to manipulate physical substances.

Those of true alchemical laboratory tradition were always aware of the fact that everything is Mind: Both alchemy and magic were approached as being intimately connected on a holistic level from that overarching mindset. Over time, different ideas sprang up that pulled away from the integrated view and focused upon isolated aspects, much like the cubicle mindset that is prevalent today: This person over here does this and that person over here does that. They all run a great big company, but none of the parts have any idea how each of the other parts works or fits into the whole.

Without the integrated lock-and-key initiatory teachings, the ideas behind the fragmented pieces of the sacred sciences basically became less and less based on direct experience, allowing for what people believed, or what they decided to believe, to become part of what was then encoded into traditions as belief systems without the inherent balance that was part of the original system. That kind of balance really did exist in the Western mysteries a long time ago yet most of the pieces were not in the hands of the uninitiated.

True initiatory streams were maintained, but they went underground right about the time of the fall of the Roman Empire, for many reasons. During the heyday of the Roman Empire, there was a lot of religious freedom; far more so than what we have today because there was no judgment of which deity to whom someone was devoted. It was a melting pot of many cultural streams coming together.

Towards the end of the Roman Empire, the Church of Rome had become, basically, the source of religious authority in that domain and had done its best to squelch its competition. The fact it spent far more time stamping out streams of competing Christianity rather than actually fighting so-called heretics and pagans is not really talked about much.

Yes, there were always wars with pagan factions for land and power, but the Church of Rome spent a good deal more effort, from a certain point of view, stamping out alternative streams of Christian belief that competed with what today has come to be accepted as original Christianity without most of its modern adherents ever having been aware that it was not always so.

At the time Roman Christianity was grafted into the Empire as the official religion there were several other versions of Christianity that were just as valid in their own right, if not more, as the version prevalent today.[3]

During the Inquisition, the initiatory streams went even further underground, and the main Hermetic disciplines of alchemy and magic were privately studied by seekers but often separately, based more on personal interest and the texts available than having a cohesive, structured education in the subject.

One of the cool things about Rome in its peak was that the Mysteries were more commonly accessible. There were always people who just wanted to be devotional, just like today, but if a person truly wanted to enter into the Mysteries and really evolve and learn, there were a lot more legitimate channels to do so then, than are available now.

We think we have evolved, and become so advanced, but really, in some ways we have taken some huge back steps. It is all in divine order, but it is interesting though to look at it and know

---

[3] The stewardship of the original initiatory, foundational teachings of the Christos that Jesus taught was, prior to the Church of Rome, actually overseen by members of his same bloodline, many of whom were also Bishops within the original Church. They were the authority in their bishoprics within that lineage because they were part of a bloodline that taught and preserved those teachings long before they had been presented to the masses, albeit in allegory most of the time. Prior to usurpation by the state, true authority over original Christianity was inherent in the bloodlines of Jesus' family, whose lineage is far more ancient than academia has yet to acknowledge, which is how he was in possession of the Mysteries now solely credited to him. In its early formation as Rome's official religion, the usurpers could do little to seize full and immediate power, but over time they succeeded in removing those with true bloodline authority, the Desposyni, from the Church. In much the same way, they later contributed to the political overthrow of monarchs of royal hereditary bloodlines and eventually usurped the complete right to crown the monarchs of Europe, which prior to Charlemagne was a power that did not rest with the papacy. (This is a very complex subject which will be dealt with directly in a separate publication.)

that what most of the magical revivalist traditions have attempted to do is to go back and figure out how to recreate processes based on Egyptian writing and fragments from the traditions that were in Greece and Rome.

That is a lot of information to digest and revivalists all have very different ideas as a result. But, the idea that we are now trying to go back and figure out what was actually understood 1,500 years ago is a little humbling when looked at from a certain point of view.

With all of our mastering the technology of seeing farther into space and doing all kinds of amazing things, the one thing that we have neglected to do is understand ourselves. Modern physicists have it down to photons and quarks. By the time that level is reached they say physicality is 99.99% empty space. Now they are coming around to looking at it in a slightly different way, but they are going to have some growing pains when they are forced to acknowledge Mind itself as the unified field.

Alchemists have always acknowledged the material aspects of the work, but they did not always have proper magical understanding. Likewise, magical practitioners did not usually have proper classical alchemical training. They were not able to understand or make progress in laboratory alchemy and thus, concocted elaborate schemes that were approached only as a psychological practice because they did not know how to do the laboratory work.

Many of them decided through human arrogance if they did not understand alchemy and could not do it, then it must not be real. Some decided it must only be psychological because all they understood of the laboratory work was that others were just trying to turn lead into gold.

For the last century many have believed that the only people who did laboratory work were those that did not understand that alchemy was really just psychological: That chemicals and ciphers were just an elaborate cover scheme. That is not true at all. There are, of course, internal components to all of these processes, but that 'psychological' notion did not come into prevalence until about a hundred years ago.

Up until then, alchemy was very laboratory-based. There were a few mystics like Jacob Boehme, people who really were opened up to mystical levels of experience. Most of them were Christian, which is very likely the only reason most of those writings and their authors survived the times in which they lived. They left records of their amazing, beautiful experiences, but they did not have practical laboratory training. They could not put their experiences in writing in context of that. They could not say, "I am having this mystical experience and that correlates with this laboratory process, or with what we learn from or see within a particular laboratory process."

Even people having these tremendous mystical experiences did not have the training in the Hermetic arts to be able to integrate them.

The truth is in the middle, in the full and proper integrated understanding of both of those branches. Alchemy has been overlooked in modern, fraternal magical teachings because it requires more effort than other practices, and because of a general lack of real understanding.

Some magical groups are embracing the idea of alchemy and doing lab work, but their only guide in doing that are the modern books published on spagyrics and plant work, that are probably not really what they are thought to be, which is illuminating and frustrating at the same time.

Even the Rosicrucian Order (AMORC), decided to downplay and phase out actual alchemical teaching. I am not sure what they do now, but they recently retained Dennis Hauck to create an alchemy museum at their headquarters. It does seem there is ongoing availability of some kind of alchemy courses, whether or not they are being taught by someone that was actually an initiate of an adept in the true, strict sense of the word or not, I do not know.

If what they are teaching for the plant work is essentially the same thing that is in the books written by Manfred Junius and Frater Albertus, those core modern founding fathers, that have just been perpetuated, then no, they are not. That is disheartening, but that is the way it is.

Even institutions that are dedicated to the recovery and integration of esoteric teachings and practices in theory, still sometimes have a conflicting agenda. AMORC became very sizable because Lewis Spence was very good at marketing. Any of the magazines that were somewhat related always had ads in the back for the correspondence courses on becoming a Rosicrucian as a member of AMORC. There is nothing wrong with that, but it is a little disconcerting to find out that the head of the Rosicrucian order could have ever been a person who would decide to downplay the teaching of practical laboratory alchemy. I find that hard to process, but yet, it is true.

The idea that alchemy was purely psychological became widespread. That viewpoint was largely adopted based on Carl Jung's influence because he did not actually know any practical laboratory alchemy. He was a psychotherapist, and he had alchemical experiences on a psychological level, but no initiatory alchemical training to put them into proper classical context. So he came up with his own theories and wrote copiously to the point where his concepts have largely overridden truly Hermetic ideas within the modern magical mindset.

Jung's predominant alchemical opinions were held by revivalist magical practitioners up until the point of Israel Regardie, who was shown otherwise by Frater Albertus. Israel Regardie was a huge player in the formative parts of modern magical theory, having released the major teachings of the Order of the Golden Dawn into the magical community, which still heavily influences much of the magical thought prevalent in the mainstream now. He was also a psychotherapist.

For a long time, he held the same opinions as Jung. His writings held similar opinions. Then Frater Albertus came along and knocked on his door. I am not sure exactly happened but by the time they were done, he had a very different opinion about laboratory alchemy. He had published *The Philosopher's Stone* originally in 1938, but a second edition was published in 1970, with an introduction where he admits to enjoying being made "to eat crow" in reference to his prior opinion of alchemy being of psychological basis only. I have the third printing of that edition from 1978, which contains the following dedication to Frater Albertus:

It gives me enormous satisfaction to dedicate this new edition
to
Frater Albertus Spagyricus
who, benevolently and sagaciously, has opened my eyes to the
further meanings of Alchemy.

I have not seen the first edition to make comparisons; however, the edition I have of *The Philosopher's Stone* has some really valuable insights, namely the first sections of the book because Israel Regardie discusses the true alchemical processes that are happening within a deeper magical context, but from a more accurate alchemical viewpoint.

Practitioners who study a lot of the Golden Dawn material or a lot of that modern Hermetic foundational magic curriculum, will talk about *The Tree of Life* and *A Garden of Pomegranates* and a lot his of other foundational works. It is unfortunate that hardly any of them even know Regardie wrote *The Philosopher's Stone*. Most of them do not know that it even exists. I find it curious that they have not read it. Yet, they are in magical traditions that are pushing alchemy around as a word, saying, "Oh, we are doing alchemy," and they are not doing alchemy. They are just using alchemy words they do not understand.

That is one of the things that happens when prominent influencers hold certain positions. Then later on, towards the end of their life, something happens and they have a total shift about that particular thing, but because that was not prevalent from the beginning throughout the core of their work, most people do not know. Then it takes a while for perceptions to shift. It is many decades later, and now it is finally slowly coming more into the forefront of awareness.

Regardie did spend the rest of his life in pursuit of laboratory alchemy and that is why he rewrote *The Philosopher's Stone*. It is likely not well known in magical circles because it has been out of print for a long time. It is likely not well known in alchemical circles because it was written by a magical person, and they often do not pay much attention to modern texts of that genre. There is still a huge rift to mend between these two predominant mindsets.

VII

Barriers in Approaching Real & Practical Alchemical Study

Once one accepts the premise that there is a real practical alchemy, there are barriers in approaching productive alchemical study. Mainly, aside from not having a specific teacher, it is access to authentic texts themselves that were written by real adepts, not just the paper mill that was pumped out for centuries. Amongst all those fraudulent texts pumped out for money, there are real texts.

How does a person, in the beginning, discern one from the other? It is quite unlikely, statistically speaking, that one person isolated, not connected to other people who know, could sift through that productively because there are just tons of it.

At one point in history, alchemy was the most published subject in the western world because of the ability to command premiums. Fake texts are 99% of what is floating around.

Then comes even more complicated territory. Aside from sheer quantity of texts, there are a number of purported paths to the Philosopher's Stone itself, coupled with difficulties in cross terminology and conceptual changes within the laboratory tradition that span more than 1,000 years. Furthermore, even if one has an authentic text written by an adept, those are the texts that are full of blinds put in to conceal and protect what they were saying.

Why is that? Because adepts did not write for the masses. They wrote for each other. When an adept reached a certain of level of understanding, he would publish. Adepts who would read what that adept published would conclude "this is an adept," and then could gauge each other. One of the principal ways in which they found each other and communicated was by what they published.

Just like magical grimoires, there were always processes left out or included but published out of sequence. If one does not know what comes first and second and third, one has no way to evaluate a text to say, "Hmm, was this guy really putting out the truth or was this one of those fake texts that people just circulated to make money?" That is a challenge that requires more than speculative opinion.

Each text itself has to be studied and interpreted holistically. Reaching outside of one adept's writing into another's and trying to understand what one is saying by blindly comparing the terms used by both, only leads to being finished before ever getting started, because adepts were writing from isolated positions.

Adepts developed their own terminologies and the way that they described things. Over a span of 1,000 years, different concepts came into play that changed the way in which things were written. When looking at two different manuscripts, that has to be taken into account, and most people do not even know where to begin. That is definitely a problem. One cannot look at something that was written 500 years before something else and then only compare the terms and figure out what exactly is being described prior to gaining practical, accurate experience.

It is not going to happen.

For instance, the acetate path is the path that I know the most about and the one that I follow. The few adepts that left writings about those operations nearly all called their components something different in terms of the primary parts and processes.

One called them the Red Fume and the White Fume. One called them Red Mercury and White Mercury. One called them Red Wine and White Wine. Older versions often contained terms that do not have the red/white naming conventions, but simply use Sulphur and Mercury, and not always with the same definitions. Just reading their original writings, and having no idea because of never having been shown the process, where one can see the Red Fume and the White Fume, it is unlikely one would have any idea what was being said. The components look different in different parts of the process.

Seeing it though, allows one to recognize why adepts called them Red Fume and White Fume, even though the Red Fume really is kind of orange. Then when looking at it in the receiver, one can see why they called them Red Wine and White Wine, because that is exactly what they look like when condensed into liquid.

Even in the same process, which they are describing accurately, they are describing components from a particular point of view in the process. Then that is how they wrote. One needs a secret decoder ring to make it through one of those texts in any sensible way. That contributes to the list of problems in assessing texts.

Then, being able to discern which path the text is about is of paramount importance because of the number of purported "paths" that are out there. Some of them may be true, legitimate paths. Many people believe that they are, but adepts that I have had the privilege of knowing have told me the same basic thing. The only path that they know of that anyone has ever really completed and successfully executed was what they referred to as the acetate path. That is a particular process, and they were referring to mineral alchemy within that path.

There are all kinds of paths in alchemy, just within the Western paths. There is the very exciting path of the Red Dragon that sounds very cool, and the Flamel path.

Path of the Red Dragon is literally using cinnabar, a red sulphide ore of chemical mercury (Hg), which is borderline insane. Yet, its use is also still very much alive in certain Eastern traditions, where they have been doing it for a long time and have found a way to deal with it.

There is Western alchemy, which is the alchemy discussed here. Then, parallel to that, there are Chinese and Indian lines of alchemy that are just as legitimate in their traditional standing as anything Western. Eastern methods are based on an entirely different kind of alchemical approach. My understanding of Eastern alchemy is very limited because my focus is on the Western Mysteries as an initiatory path. With the Eastern traditions being so centered around chemical mercury, attempting that work without the direct oversight of an accomplished adept from those traditions is quite foolish.

If one is going to study and practice under someone that is truly an adept or master, one will learn what they are teaching. If they are teaching how to make an actual, real quintessence out of mercury, then great because a master is at the helm. That is very different from running around thinking it can be figured out on one's own and dying of mercury vapor, because it is very toxic.

41

Aside from that, then there is the Flamel path. Nicholas Flamel is the most famous documented Western alchemist. He was a real person. He was a scrivener, notary, and bookseller in the 1300's. To shortcut the story, at some point he ended up funding hospitals and churches, renovating churches and building cemeteries, and doing all kinds of things a regular, simple bookseller would never have had the money to do. He set up all kinds of charities. He is still renowned in France today as part of its national history. Even though the French cannot explain it, they acknowledge him. People come up with all kinds of theories about he got all that gold and how he gave staggering amounts of money to charity. Some like to point out that his wife Perenelle had been twice widowed and had some wealth, but her modest wealth would have had to have been legendary prior to accomplishing all that they did together, and it was not. Even today, the wealth they gave to charity would be staggering amounts of money.

The explanation that he gives in his own writings, in his own hand, are that eventually he figured out an alchemical process based on a book called *The Book of Abraham* that he was able to buy for the token of 2 florins or something ridiculously inexpensive. It took him 30 years to understand the book. Then he and his wife did the work together because she was just as involved in it as he was.

We have legitimacy there, and the high likelihood that it is indeed a true path to the Philosopher's Stone. The problem though, with that particular path, is that people get up to a certain point in it, and then they all stop because nobody knows what the step is after that.

The first stage of that work ends up with a material called the Star Regulus of Antimony. Alchemists have been fascinated with it for centuries. Achieving that stage of the work has become so prominent that there are pictures of it online. Anyone can look it up on Google and see it, but that is where it stops. The process after that point is a complete enigma. Instead of pursuing an alternative path, those dedicated to it just keep spinning their wheels. It is a glass ceiling. I am sure somewhere, there are adepts who know the rest of that path, but they are not talking.

Then there are various other paths: The dew path, rainwater path, gur work, the urine path, all kinds of other paths that have been created because of certain texts, several having only pictures. Some of the ideas may be valid, but even if so, most would require a tremendous amount more work because of the quantity of starting material one would need to have to succeed in those processes, which is probably part of what is left out of those kinds of texts. If one is attempting to emulate macrocosmic forces, and using natural substances easily collected as a result of those forces, then it is also to be reasonably expected that the quantity of material one would need to obtain and properly process would be a staggering amount of work. Armand Barbault's *Gold of a Thousand Mornings* is a great example illustrating my point.

One of the things an alchemist comes to understand is any natural, complete organic substance has the three philosophical Principals within it (or the four philosophical Elements). It must or the material would decompose: In fact, it is the separation of the philosophical Principals that brings about the condition we call death.

It is not that one cannot make a quintessence out of any natural organic material. It is just a question of how much of it one would need in order to be able to get enough of the portions of philosophical materials that would be required to make any real progress. There are a lot of mechanical considerations of sheer proportion that can make some processes really impractical, even if they are technically correct.

To me, many of those kinds of paths just offer really labor-intensive busywork and no payoff when compared to other paths that will lead one to obtaining a real quintessence of some kind, though perhaps not from the kingdom to which one may aspire when first starting on the path.

I do not believe that the urine path is actually a real path for what I think are pretty good reasons, even though there are plenty of people out there promoting it. Yes, it is a natural substance, but it is a waste product, not necessarily a complete thing that has all the philosophical Principals in it. It has been broken down and separated by the body and other components of what was originally ingested in order to get urine as a byproduct, have been taken and used elsewhere.

Urine is not a complete thing, for the purposes of alchemy. I do think that it has been effectively used a solvent because of its acid. Clearly, it has health properties because the American Indians used it for a long time, and they still do because of its endorphin content. However that may be, as a foundational material for creating a quintessence, I do not think so. I have never seen any evidence to the contrary.

Furthermore, texts used by those who purport the urine path use the term 'Golden Water' quite plainly, which should be the first clue that the starting material is NOT the obvious. In some advanced alchemy work, there is a 'Golden Water' obtained from a process using a mineral, which is likely the material referred to in those texts, but this fact is either unknown or conveniently overlooked by those promoting the urine path as something of substance.

VIII

Other Barriers to the Work

Other barriers to productive practical work are modern theories that are being piled on top of the whole process that do not actually have any ancient premise for the work, or at least not a properly understood premise for the work; like astrology, which makes things very complicated.

Some modern teachers, unfortunately, required their students to learn how to do incredibly complicated astrological charts for timing alchemical processes. Frater Albertus was very much oriented toward thinking astrological timing was somehow important, and he was not the only one. Most of those who were his core students still hold that line of thought, often teaching it as an aspect of practical necessity in the work.

I have never given consideration to astrology as being useful in laboratory alchemy work because of adept training in deep magic having clearly demonstrated that astrology made no discernible difference. It stood to reason in my mind, that if it made no difference to real magic, it would make no difference in real alchemy either. However, since many others have adopted it, or have tried to integrate it into practical alchemical work, which causes nothing but hindrance, it is important to understand why it is a barrier to productive work.

Getting into the problems of basing any practical work on

astrological calculation, it is fortunate that it can actually be circumvented because it opens an entire can of worms. It is such a huge can of worms that I am often reticent to discuss it because people do not want to hear that what circulates as Western, tropical astrology is its own creation.

There is nothing really alchemically useful in astrology other than the archetypes themselves and understanding their functions. They may have occasionally been applied as ciphers within texts by authors who may have used that allegorical method of concealment, or at least wanted it to appear they were concealing something real.

Basic understanding of archetypes is tremendously valuable, but the calculation of charts in order to determine a favorable time and place to create a quintessence or do particular lab work, or any magical work for that matter, is nothing but a big crapshoot because there are a whole bunch of assumptions that come into play. Most people do not realize they are assumptions, much less know where or how those 'rules' originated.

Basically, 1,700 years ago was the last time the tropical ephemeris really lined up with where the stars actually were because Ptolemy VI of Egypt, a Greek pharaoh, was the last one to do it. When he did it, he fudged a few things because even he said the calculations were too complicated. Part of the reason was because he was Greek and the Egyptians did not teach him everything because they did not want him to know. They did not trust Greeks.

What we have handed down from Ptolemy VI as how things worked in the Egyptian system was a bit of a bastardization from the very beginning. Only nobody really knew that. Who would have known that? That is one major problem.

46

Then we have to contrast tropical astrology with sidereal astrology. Eastern astrology has always been sidereal (which is based upon where the celestial bodies actually are). Western astrology for a long time was based only upon the tropical ephemeris. There is now, over the last few decades, a movement in Western astrology toward its own sidereal system. In fact, it is mainly magical practitioners in Hermetic-based traditions that are aware of the importance between the two types of ephemerides. Magical practitioners who strive towards planetary magic of many kinds all want their workings to be as successful as possible, and therefore have gone to lengths to make sure they know where the planets actually are when they do that work. Serious occultists use the sidereal ephemeris because they know the difference; something the more mainstream metaphysical community does not want to acknowledge.

The problem with the tropical ephemeris is it does not take into account the Precession of the Equinoxes, which the sidereal systems have always accounted for, as did the Egyptians. What that means is every 72 years, there is a 1-degree slip in the zodiac from where it would be calculated to be by simple math versus where it actually is. The problem is very similar to why we use a leap year in our modern calendar: A year is not 365 days, it is 365-1/4 days.

When you extend that 1-degree slip every 72 years out over 1,700 years, it becomes a 24-degree slip. Tropically, my sun is in Gemini. Sidereally, my sun is in Taurus. It is a big difference. Unless one's sun sign is all the way at the end of one zodiac sign in its last 6 degrees so that it will not slide over to the next sign, most sun signs are not really where they are thought to be, which is really kind of disconcerting.

How did this happen? It is the perfect example of ancient

understanding being lost and the modern world taking a long time to catch up. The ancient initiates knew about the Precession of the Equinoxes; however, that was not rediscovered in the modern world until the 1970's. In the interim the planetary placement was just calculated out mathematically as though there were no slip to account for, because no one knew any better. But, in that interim, what is called Western tropical astrology had already become institutionalized with its own set of processes, practices, and belief systems.

Objectively looking, not at the sidereal interpretation of astrology, but just where the stars themselves are, they are where the sidereal ephemeris says, not the tropical ephemeris.

I have had this conversation with tropical astrologers and they utterly reject what their Hermetic magical practitioner cousins could have told them some time ago. But, aside from their emotional investment in what some believe is an unbroken chain of ancient wisdom, and because they found ways to interpret the signs and archetypes in ways that line up with what they feel they see on the outside as an accurate reflection of those attributes, they are anchored in tropical astrology.

Despite how ancient most modern astrologers would like to believe their version of astrology is, wishing to graft that ancientness onto what they do and believe, tropical astrology itself is a fairly modern reinvention created by revivalists with good intentions who simply did not have all the facts.

Now that being said, Western sidereal astrology has got similar problems. It has a leg up on knowing where the planets actually are, but at the same time, all the rest of it is stuff that has been made up to try to make sense of all the rest of it.

Unfortunately, at least currently as far as I am aware, there is really no middle ground in Western astrology because even if one accepts the issue with the ephemerides being different, and makes a logical decision to use the sidereal ephemeris for planetary positions, there are huge differences in interpretation between the systems as well. Someone who wishes to practice Western astrology, retaining their understanding of archetypes and houses, etc., but wishes to use data from a sidereal ephemeris is probably going to have to learn to do natal charts and transits by hand, and then do their own chart interpretations, instead of pushing a button on a $300 program, or a free website, that spits out a natal chart and boilerplate interpretations.

There are Western sidereal astrology programs, but then one is forced to be required to use the rest of what those who created the program have decided is correct. Western sidereal astrology does not use a house system, only the zodiac signs and planets themselves, to cite one example.

I do not want to belabor the subject of astrology, only focus on it enough to shed some light on the problems with using it in conjunction with practical alchemy, and by extension, magic. Modern astrology, as a distant cousin of the Hermetic arts, is a revivalist tradition trying to find its way, because the way the Egyptians did it was lost. Revivalism is great, but rigidity in revivalism, where major issues are ignored for decades instead of embraced, pushing away what would strengthen knowledge instead of suppressing it, does not lead to illumination.

If an accurate natal chart cannot reliably be created, then neither can an accurate chart for anything else. The complexity of the problem is not a secret. Anyone at any point in history that became an astrologer that learned how to do calculations would eventually run into places where the system did not work, and then that would force them to come up with a sequence of fudge factors of how one might try to account for and deal with the issue.

One of the ways magical people dealt with the problem was by coming up with shorthand systems, such as days of the week and magical hours, etc. This leads to rulership charts where Sunday is ruled by the sun and the first hour after sunrise is the hour of the sun; then the next hour is ruled by the next planet in sequence, and so on.

Those concepts were all made up basically because everybody said, "The math is too complicated. I do not want to do it, but I need to create a shorthand system that works, or that I feel works for me." Hundreds and hundreds of years later, people are just republishing these tables and books, telling people, "This is how it really is." Just because Agrippa wrote it down, and everyone plagiarized from him, does not make it true. It is shameful really, that those who are supposedly teaching 'real' magic could just write and publish books on magic as though they were grade-school book reports, without any obvious signs of actual self-possessed thinking.

Even if what Agrippa wrote were really true, how do we know that Tuesday is actually Tuesday? If Tuesday really is ruled by Mars, prove to me that Tuesday is Tuesday. I have only thought of one way in which at least one of the days of the week could be reasonably assured, and that is not how we run our calendar.

The only day that could be 'proven' from simple observation is Monday, by starting on a full moon, and saying Monday is on a full moon and calculating everything out after that because every 28 days, there is an even 4-week cycle. Then at least true Monday, if indeed there is such a thing, could be identified. Even that though, only really pegs one out of seven days. The days of the week as they are currently named do not follow the sequential order of the planets that are their Roman namesakes, so there is still no real solution. There is no way around this dilemma.

The cool thing is, based on true alchemical teaching, it does not matter. Many modern alchemists will probably reel in horror at that statement, but it is true because the *Emerald Tablet* teaches that alchemy is done with One Thing; not one thing plus astrological timing, or one thing plus our own personal juju pushed in there, or moonbeams, or anything else. One Thing.

Alchemists do not add stuff. They simply remove what is superfluous to the perfection of the One Thing. That is a little high level. They basically have to break it down, separate it, purify out what is superfluous, and then recombine it in a particular way. That is the process of alchemy, the Royal Art. That is how a quintessence is made.

Being able to bypass all the fluff that has been put on top of original alchemy teaching really is very liberating. I never bought into any of it because I always had the argument, "Prove to me Tuesday is Tuesday." For the last 20 years, that has been my argument. I also had the same nagging feelings about the Albertus version of most of the plant work taught in his *prima* classes. I just did not know why I felt so strongly about that back then, aside from the astrological part of his teaching. I could not quite put my finger on it then. I have a really good filter for knowing when something is not right, even if I do not know what the answer is at that time, I know when something is off base. That helps me navigate through things.

Being able to learn alchemy liberated from astrological calculation is something for which all aspiring alchemists should be quite grateful. In the past, many did believe in the necessity of celestial configurations to be able to do alchemy work, so some of them would wait months or years to be able to try a process because they believed that it would not work, and the materials were precious enough to come by that working against the stars seemed unwise.

Adepts know that is not true, but they have allowed the modern, mainstream occult, alchemical community to continue thinking that it is, because basically, until somebody really gets that, they probably do not have enough Understanding to be able to do real alchemy anyway. In their mindset it really does not change the net effect. To a certain point I agree that is true, but how long will it take to shift mindsets if no one is willing to teach more than surface level *regurgita*?

I have a problem with the whole notion of allowing disinformation to be perpetuated. If I am not going to teach something, or I am going to put boundaries on what I am willing to teach and what I am not willing to teach, then I will state it: "Yes, I am going to teach that. No, I am not going to teach that." What I will not do is participate in the perpetuation of disinformation to totally screw people up when sincerely seeking a deeper spiritual path, by deciding for them that they are not ready because they currently are not able to grok the deepest level of understanding. That is why the path of learning to create quintessences exists, to gradually prepare and expand consciousness that allows one to grasp understanding that was initially beyond one's reach.

We all have to pay our dues. We have all been hazed by the universe, but there some aspects of the manner in which aspects of the Western Mystery Tradition are currently taught that are either predatory or unnecessary. Some of that comes from a longstanding tradition of extreme secrecy based on being in an age where that was required for survival. But today, more often than not, it is simply a thinly veiled cover for substituting control mechanisms in place of actual dissemination of substantial teaching.

At a certain point, it needs to be revisited: "Are we doing this because we are elitists and we do not want people to know?" Some esotericists are elitists. Or, "Are we doing it because we are just dragging around some old notions that no longer serve the greater good?" Personally I err on the side of caution, for the most part, which I think is a fairly prudent concept. That is why I state my position as clearly as possible on such matters.

IX

Difficulty of the Great Work in the Metallic Kingdom

Practical alchemy work is always said to start with the *Prima Materia*. The vast majority of the time it has been stated, and the idea has been promoted, that the *Prima Materia* has never been identified. That is a blind because it is not true. Another thing that has been generally misunderstood about that idea is that the *Prima Materia* is not a substance, it is a state or a condition of being of a substance.

When some adept texts make references about the *Prima Materia* and having to go and find it, what they are talking about is the crude material that is used to start the work. That material then taken and brought into a certain condition, and that condition is what alchemists call the *Prima Materia*. That condition can be made out of any complete, natural substance. Whether or not that substance is particularly conducive to get results that alchemists want because of the amount of the natural philosophical Principals within it, is a whole different thing. *Prima Materia* is said to be everywhere but that people do not recognize it, and that is true because it is in everything that is natural.

It is the fact that the crude matter is not in the condition by which alchemy proceeds from that point, in the state that it is found, because that is part of the process of learning how to reverse it back into its base philosophical Elements, also called 'Chaos of the Elements,' that causes confusion. What the substance is before it comes into being the thing that it is when one finds it, is the state one has to know how to reverse it back to, in order to be able to separate the philosophical Elements, purify them, and put them back together again. There is a lot of misunderstanding about that whole idea, which was done on purpose; quite frankly it was pretty brilliant. Those adepts were pretty smart.

It is identifying the starting material in the advanced work that is where seekers have been stumped for forever, which is why there are all kinds of purported alchemical paths. The truth is, if it is a complete natural substance, it can be decomposed back to its *Prima Materia* state. It is just that certain substances are known to be more useful in making progress from that point than others, but it is not that any one of them does not have *Prima Materia*.

In the metallic work, in the path to the Philosopher's Stone using an acetate method, texts referring to *Prima Materia* are really talking about the process to get to the Green Lion, which has all kinds of names and depictions. One of the most famous depictions is often described as the 'Green Lion Devouring the Sun.' The funny thing about that epithet is that there are a lot of modern alchemists who have commented on that picture and simply repeated the title that other people have said, but they clearly have not ever actually seen the process itself because then they would know the Green Lion is NOT devouring the sun. Part of the reason this misconception persists is because there is more than one version of that image that was created in the past. Some of the images are far more insightful than others because they actually show all of the philosophical Elements (if one knows what they are), whereas many others do not.

This Green Lion image[4] above is one with complete symbolism. There is the Green Lion with seven Stars in his body. He is standing upright, and there is a Sun just slightly overhead and a Moon that is partially submerged in the Water, along with a lot more going on in this picture than appears at first glance. If one really understands what the Green Lion is and what is done to it, then one understands it is not devouring the Sun. The Sun is coming out of the Green Lion, and so is the Moon, the water, the Earth itself covered in foliage, and all the other things present in the picture. Because many do not understand the process of what is done with the Green Lion, they do not know what they are looking at, and thus, they have named it the opposite of what it actually is.

---

[4] J.D. Mylius. "The Green Lion." In Philosophia Reformata. Frankfurt, 1622. Hand-colored reproduction. Adam McLean. http://www.alchemywebsite.com/amclglr3.html

The name keeps being regurgitated without any real thought or understanding. It is a key thing. Those who put that in a book and call it by that epithet without commenting on the fact that is not actually really what is happening, sends a clear signal to me that they probably do not really have the alchemical understanding to be writing a book. It is disconcerting and it significantly reduces the number of people one can actually talk to about real alchemy.

The whole point of talking to someone who teaches is to learn something from them and if there are clear signals that they do not understand the practical basics, there is just no point in having the conversation. The number of people to whom one can talk to and learn something gets significantly smaller every rung up the ladder. It gets more and more difficult to come by accurate esoteric knowledge.

Once one knows what the Green Lion is made from the advanced work can start. It is not really that difficult. The Green Lion could be made next week, that is not the problem. The problem once it is obtained is knowing how to accelerate the evolution of the Green Lion into the Red Lion.

The Red Lion is the Philosopher's Stone under another name. This is where the name the Great Work comes about. Taking the right quantity of the Green Lion without purifying anything, without doing anything else to it other than keeping it in a molten state (three hundred-ish degrees centigrade) for several years, without interruption of the heat, the result should be the basis of the Red Lion.[5]

---

[5] Technically, I say 'basis' because there is also a ferment that is added at a specific point in the process, in order to determine the nature of the Stone, but that is a complex subject that is outside the scope of this brief work.

Stop and consider the amount of labor involved with that process hundreds of years ago. Even today the problems are power outages, or if one succeeds in keeping it at that level of heat for years, the electric bill. The modern age has its conveniences but it is not without its challenges unless one is financially well-heeled and can afford to create a system that really will make sure there are no power interruptions; which would require advanced backup systems in general, and even then there is no guarantee because at a certain point all those systems can run out of power. If that happens what is obtained is a lovely solidified chunk of green vitrified glass.

The Great Work is about learning how to take the Green Lion and separate it into its philosophical Elements, purify each of the them, and then put them back together again to circulate and eventually become One Thing. That work dramatically reduces the amount of time the process takes because impurities are removed. The other way without separation and purification, the impurities are still in there so the small portions that get perfected must then act on the rest to overcome impurities. If the impurities have been taken out, there is less for the pure philosophical Elements to overcome, and the process can accelerate faster. That is really all alchemy is doing; taking out the substances that cause something to stop evolving.

Alchemy accelerates evolution though alchemists themselves are not doing it: It is the substance that has the evolution inherent within it. Everything has that function, and the reason things stop evolving at a certain point is because there is a function in the universe that brings that about, otherwise, there would be no differentiation. There would not be a physical anything, there would not be a multiplicity, and there would be no environment in which to evolve. It is a vital part of the evolutionary process towards the end of a person's cycle of incarnations, that one becomes aware of these ideas and then begins the Great Work. There are forces embedded in nature that accelerate that, if one learns how to uncover them and how to apply them; that is alchemy.

The Red Lion, the Philosopher's Stone, is the pinnacle of alchemical quintessences: It is the Universal Medicine. It is as accomplished in the terms of creating a quintessence as one is going to get. Now there are all kinds of other things that can be done with it after that, but that is a whole other discussion. One reason why it is called the Great Work is because there are a lot of obstacles in the advanced mineral work. The salts do not volatize easily, and there are tricks and secrets to learn in order to make certain processes work. One can get stumped on that for years, and some alchemists never find their way past that threshold.

X

True Initiatory Levels in Alchemy & Magic

Adepts have said that either one must have a teacher or have the intercession of divine inspiration, which basically means instruction from a nonphysical intelligence. Either way one still has to have a teacher, or be taught by someone who had a teacher that was an adept, to get to a certain point where one can then pick up one's own inner teacher. Either way much of it is not intuitive; in fact, it is actually counter intuitive so it is very difficult to say, "Oh, I can just try to figure it out." That is highly unlikely without some kind of proper instruction; however, incredibly intelligent people still set about attempting to force the lower mind into deciphering how the enigma of alchemy is solved, and fail continuously. It is not necessarily about intellect, though that is useful, it is only a part of the issue.

Another part of it is, if this is not the lifetime where one is supposed to succeed in the Art, it is not going to happen: It is up to one's Higher Genius. The Higher Genius is the one that determines how many incarnations one has and whether enough has been learned for what is needed to be able to complete that level—to fulfill one's capacity as a human being and evolve to the next level. The Higher Genius is the one orchestrating that.

If one is not ready to complete the work all the way through to the Philosopher's Stone, one can still complete portions of the work. If one has evolved far enough, developing the ability to communicate and negotiate with the Higher Genius and say, "Okay, what do I have to do?" becomes possible. Basically, it is an alignment process. There is an alignment and a surrendering of personal will, which is basically the only real use of personal will that is actually useful: To surrender it to the Higher Genius of one's own free will.

Most everything else people run around thinking they are doing with their will is really just getting in their way. A lot of people have figured that out, but they have not really figured out what to do about it. It is because they have not been taught to communicate with the Higher Genius, in a way that is very certain that it is really the Higher Genius. A lot of people talk to a lot of things, though they are not necessarily the higher aspects of what they think they are. I am not saying they are not, I am just saying there is a protocol for how those things are dealt with in proper training to be certain, and many have not had access to that level of training.

So that directs one's journey into true initiatory levels in alchemy and magic. It is the same process in the inner alchemical work as it is in the outer laboratory work. They are both long, arduous, and difficult. One does not think, "Oh, I am just going to float around in the ethers in my imagination and I am just going to visualize that I have done the Great Work and then because I have done a visualization that is really what is going to happen." It does not work that way. Though those skills may be used at certain times, if it were as 'intuitive' as all those who claim to have deep intuition would like to believe, many more people would have a far more accurate understanding of real alchemy.

The outer work is sometimes more intuitive than the inner work, from a certain point of view. Effectiveness in these things requires initiation on some level. In alchemy and magic, the way it was taught to me and the definitions that I have come to accept because of the way they make sense to me, are as follows:

A **master alchemist** is a person that has achieved production of the true Philosopher's Stone. He can perform all of the works with which the Stone can be made to do. He could not have achieved production of it unless he understood all of the aspects of the work that are required in order to be able to do that.

A **master magician** has achieved full union with his Higher Genius and can perform all the works that can be achieved from that state of consciousness. The master magician has learned the inner work; however, just because he has learned the inner work does not mean he just automatically knows how to do the outer work when he gets to a certain level. He might have a better idea, but unless he has been directly taught he does not really know the specifics.

The same thing happens to the master alchemist, the difference being that the alchemist has the Philosopher's Stone from which is made the Elixir of Life, which when ingested connects one to those powers (extensions of the Higher Genius). So he does not need to go learn all the inner mechanics that the magical seeker had to learn in order to become a master. That is because those aspects come about as a by-product of ingesting the elixir made from the Stone itself; that is what the Stone does, or rather, that is part of what it does.

The odd thing is, that of the handful of people that have possessed the Stone, of the writings that were left, many who obtained the Stone did not know how to make the Elixir of Life from it. Naturally those who just found or stole the Stone spent far more time transmuting metal and trying to impress persons of state, and then ended up getting locked in towers because when they ran out of projection powder (the Stone ground down into a powder) and did not know how to make more, those persons of state were no longer amused.

Even amongst real alchemists, just because someone acquired the Stone does not automatically mean they knew how to make the Elixir of Life out of it. That is the only way to be able to extend life and longevity, and not knowing how to do it can result in premature death. The Stone is basically pure God dwelling in a physical substance.

Ingesting too much God at one time is bad for the nervous system. The body will shut down and that is the universe's way of keeping idiots from getting further than they should, even if they are alchemists: If they still have not gotten that dosage is something that really needs to be paid careful attention, they are still idiots as far as the universe is concerned, no matter if they are smarter than 99% of the people on the planet. It is all relative.

An **adept alchemist** has been instructed by a master or within the master's lineage under another adept, possesses full keys to the work, is a true initiate, and is in the process of working towards completion of the Stone. Now, possesses 'full keys to the work' does not mean that every single thing has been spelled out in painful detail. More like nothing has been left out of the explanation in mostly broad strokes, and then some finer strokes, but there are things one is going to have to figure out. It is not just going to get handed over without real work.

Same thing with the **adept magician** who has been instructed by a master or within the master's lineage under another adept, possesses full keys to the work, is a true initiate, and is in the process of working towards completion of union with the Higher

Genius. Again possesses full keys to the work is broad strokes, not every little thing is spelled out.

The **initiate alchemist** has received instruction from an adept as a direct student, has been taught the correct overall process of the work, been given most of the keys (not all), has been brought through specific training that affects his consciousness, and is working towards adepthood through confection of quintessences which bring about integrations of consciousness that allow communication with aspects of the Higher Genius.

An **initiate magician** has received instruction from an adept as a direct student, has been taught the correct overall process of the work and been given most of the keys (not all), has been brought through specific training that affects consciousness, and is working towards adepthood through specific inner work processes which bring about integrations of consciousness that allow one to communicate with aspects of the Higher Genius.

There is no way to circumvent the necessity to learn to properly communicate with one's Higher Genius to evolve spiritually. It is a barrier placed by Nature. That gives a framework for understanding, from this particular Hermetic point of view, what the true initiatory stages and steps are. It is not about self-dedicating and doing a little ceremony; there is not much of that in real alchemy and even in real magical work there is honestly very little of that.

Studying under an adept is really more like: "This is the way it is, and this is what you need to know. Now go do it." There is a little bit more in the explanations, but there is no pomp and circumstance. True adepts care little for pageantry. It is up to the pupil to do the work after that. If one does not make any progress, then the adept just does not pay attention anymore. Time spent on someone who is not really serious is just time spent away from everything else. Adepts have to prioritize their time just like everyone else.

That gives a framework for both the magical and alchemical traditions, and the way that they parallel each other. It is important to really have a clear understanding of that. When I speak or teach using those terms, those are the definitions that I use.

XI

Understanding the Beginning Work in Practical Alchemy

What is taught now as traditional plant alchemy is really a modern revival, sort of a best stab at recreating a classical process by Frater Albertus. It goes through all the motions, and seems like in theory it should be correct, but it is not really deep alchemy. It is only taught by modern adepts to learn basic mechanics.

So how did I come to this point of view? Well, I am an accredited Master Herbalist (that is worth about as much as the paper it can be printed on, but it is an accreditation) and I created and ran an aromatherapy company for a long time. I had vats and vats of essential oils, in addition to making herbal tinctures and other natural products. I was around a lot of those materials, and in distilling and doing all those things while working through processes specifically taught as plant alchemy, that little bell in my head that always goes off when something is not right, was always nagging at me.

That went on for years and I could never pinpoint what it was that was not right, because on the surface it looks like it should be correct. No one can fault someone for thinking that it is, because really it is a very sound explanation. Except that there are a couple holes in it and one has to really come to maturity with the ideas about alchemy to start finding the holes in it. What I ended up coming to is that what is taught and published as modern plant alchemy is not what people think: It is really a species of advanced herbalism. There is nothing wrong with advanced herbalism, but passing it off as alchemy is like calling a cat a dog as far as I am concerned.

They are not the same thing. The telltale sign is that a lot of people never really progress out of plant alchemy; but, even if one does not there is still a whole world of plant work to explore, and a quintessence is a quintessence. It will, can, and should do certain things, and if it does not it is not really a quintessence. I have known countless practicing laboratory alchemists that have spent years tinkering away in their labs thinking that they are creating plant quintessences, true spagyric remedies, and the products they make do not do anything.

Now, a lot of people can just accept that because they have not had a contrasting experience in their own paradigm that lets them know that there is something missing. I was fortunate enough to be taught by four adepts in the course of my life, for whatever the reasons are. Two of them were Western magical, one of them was Eastern, and one of them was a Western alchemist. There were lots of unconnected dots for me before the alchemist. I had lots and lots of pieces, yet did not have a full working template that made sense to me even though I spent years and years digging and researching. I had a library that would fill up an entire large wall.

Eventually I had enough pieces that with a little bit of help from a real alchemist, all those dots could then be made into a picture. The dots were all pixels that just needed to be rearranged to make a coherent picture and I did not have to bang my head on the wall anymore. Before that though, the only reason I had the tenacity to dig after that level of knowledge was because prior to studying alchemy, I had actually seen real magic.

With my first teacher there were times I wondered if he was completely crazy or not, but he could demonstrate power: Real stuff that most people would never believe could ever happen in the physical. That is what gave me the conviction of knowing that magic was actually real. He passed when I was still very young, but if it had not have been for him I may not have had the paradigm shift to separate the false from the true either. After his demonstrations, I knew that there was real magic in magic, so there had to be real magic in alchemy. That was my line of thought and I have held to that ever since.

XII

Ideas Circulating About Plant Alchemy & Spagyrics

Most of the Albertus plant work that is taught has never sat right with me. I understood the theory and I understood the mechanics of what was being said, and what things were labeled as, but the products that were resulting did not do what adepts said quintessences were supposed to do. So I set about trying to figure out why. That led me more into magical study than it did alchemical study at that time because in modern alchemical literature there was not much of anything published that was reliable. It was not until later that I was able to connect those dots, but it turns out that my intuition was correct.

What modern plant alchemy follows is what Frater Albertus taught, which was a revivalist reconstruction in accordance with classical Elemental theory that looks correct and logical but is only a surface level of understanding. Albertus was a master, at least by the end of his life, which I mentioned before, but he did not have a corresponding plant alchemy path using the same process as the mineral work. He just did not have that. There is one, but he was not aware of it during his lifetime (or he never revealed the notion openly), so he created one that seems very logical and that is what his modern adherents teach as classical plant alchemy.

Traditional Albertus plant alchemy, basically, works off the idea of three philosophical Principals. This is something handed down by Paracelsus. Before that, there were phases in alchemy where adepts talk about the four philosophical Elements, and before that there were phases of alchemy where they only talk about two Principals. It depends on the viewpoint because they all have the same source, but classical Albertus alchemy is based around nomenclatures of philosophical Sulphur, philosophical Mercury, and philosophical Salt.

There are a number of different ways to do this work, but the idea is to get three philosophical Principals from whichever process is used. What is obtained in this process in the plant work are: the Sulphurs, which are basically the fixed and volatile oils; the Mercury portion is the *spiritus*, or ethanol alcohol from a plant; and then the Salts are the plant salts, often called potash.

There are a number of 'shortcuts' in several of the Albertus-style processes, in addition to a somewhat longer route which is more alchemically correct. In the longer, what one could do in the Albertus process would be to distill out the essential oil from the plant material and obtain the volatile aromatics (essential oil).[6] This would be the volatile aspect of the Sulphur. Then take the plant materials and put them in water, add some yeast (and possibly sugar), and allow the carbohydrates in the plant material to be converted into alcohol. This having been accomplished, then one has obtained the Mercury portion. The remaining plant matter, called feces, is then calcined down into pure white plant Salts, often called potash.

---

[6] This process is mainly used on plant materials with volatile compounds that can be separated as essential oils, thereby limiting the number of plants that can really be used in this process with any degree of success.

The plant salts are mostly potassium carbonate. Every plant has slightly different minerals, but vast majority is potassium carbonate, so its salts are called potash. That is the philosophical Salt principal. In that Salt principal are also the salts from what are called the fixed Sulphurs that did not come over from steam distillation, from the plant resins. Those salts are an extremely important part of the alchemical theory, but in this process they end up mixed in with all the other salts instead of being able to purify them separately.

Then each of these principals has to be purified, the alcohol has to be distilled at least seven times just to get it to a high enough proof to where it is pure enough to be rectified (made completely dry). The salts have to be calcined down until they are at least white. Some people do not even do that, they calcine them down until they are gray because they say they do not want to destroy the life force in them, because they do not understand deeper alchemical processes.

This superfluous life force idea has been completely forced into alchemy, just like astrology, and promotes the idea that vitality is the result of lifeforce, which is not alchemically correct. Though, many of those who contributed heavily to the formative beliefs of what has now been inherited as 'modern alchemical' teaching in the last 60 years did themselves hold those opinions. If one really understands what is written in the *Emerald Tablet*, even on a basic level, one understands that there is no life force in the equation. Life force is a result of the three philosophical Principals coming together: That conjoining is what life itself IS. There is no separate thing that is life force, but a lot of people attempting to practice alchemy are still believing that. It really interrupts true alchemical work because not purifying the salts down to at least white means they are not pure, and if one has not purified each of the principals one will never get them to fully conjoin in any kind of reasonable time frame. Ever. It will

71

not happen.

People are doing this and not purifying all the way, putting everything back in the bottle, shaking it up, thinking that they are going to create a spagyric, and then trying to take it as a remedy. Really all they have is some volatile essential oil, some alcohol, and some unpurified plant salts, which in and of themselves are really not meant to be ingested.

Until these three things are made back into One Thing that did not previously exist, that is not a quintessence. Unless it has been made into a quintessence, it is still just a bunch of plant salts in a solution of alcohol and essential oil. So then people take that and say, "Oh, I feel something." And yes, they do. What they feel is the results of alcohol entering their system, the mental buzz from the plant salts which can be toxic if they are not dealt with properly, and essential oil depending on what plant was used. That is what they are feeling. It is not because it is a quintessence, because nothing truly profound ever happens.

This has been going on for over 40 years and nobody is saying anything about it because God forbid, someone contradict tradition, right? In theory though, what is supposed to happen is that everything is absolutely purified, put all back together again, and then circulated through gentle heat process that allows each of the three philosophical Principals to eventually wed each other and create a completely new homogeneous substance—the One Thing.

That means when it is distilled over, there are not a bunch of salts left in the bottom; everything comes over. It is One Thing then. If one distills it over and it separates out, it is not one thing, and there is no way in hell it is quintessence. The amount of work required to make that happen is substantial. Well worth it, but substantial.

The reason I point this out is because there are companies out there run by practicing 'alchemists' who have bought into this whole Albertus plant alchemy theory and they sell 'pure' spagyric essences for relatively inexpensive prices. When one starts to calculate the costs of materials, time, energy, electricity, oopses in the lab (broken glassware), etc., one can pretty much bank that what is being purchased inexpensively is not a quintessence. It is a really fancy herbal tincture. If it were being sold as a really fancy herbal tincture that would be okay. Some of them are sold as 'full spectrum' extracts, indicating that the plant salts have been added back into the tincture. Ironically, that is just announcing that they are not actually spagyrics— they are not true quintessences. If the 'spagyrics' being offered online were actually real it could be a major problem. Currently, the only real problem is that what is being sold is not really what people (sellers and buyers alike) think.

This is where one runs into a major theme in the alchemy community where plant alchemy is normally called spagyrics. Spagyrics is kind of looked at by people in the alchemy community who are really more partial to the ideas in the mineral work, as not being real alchemy. On one hand, because of the way it is being taught, they are right. On the other hand they are saying spagyrics is only plant alchemy, not real alchemy, and that is not right because Paracelsus was very clear about it: *Spagyrium* is *alchemium*. It is the same thing, it is the same mechanism.

The problem is not that spagyrics is not alchemy, nor is the problem that plant alchemy is not real alchemy. The problem is those doing Albertus plant alchemy are not doing real alchemy period, but nobody has ever questioned that! The instructions were so complete and the tradition is long standing, from the modern viewpoint, so no one ever questions any of that.

What caused me to reconcile my intuition about Albertus plant alchemy was being shown there is another plant work path, and that path actually corresponds to the path that Albertus did teach in the mineral work. So, there is another way. The problem with the Albertus plant path is that the *spiritus* (ethanol) is not in the starting substance. Hermetic adepts taught that there is no need to add anything, only to carefully take away, but alcohol is not in the plant material. What has to be added?

Yeast (and sometimes sugar to feed the yeast) is added to the process to obtain this material that is supposed to be universal plant mercury which should already be present in some form. The adepts were very clear, it is not necessary to add anything to the process, so they both cannot be true. Ethanol is a plant mercury from a certain point of view, but it is not what should be called a philosophical Mercury; there is a difference far beyond mere semantics. There is a whole other way of looking at this concept which gives validation to the idea that the Albertus methods are not the most useful approach to plant alchemy.

There are adepts, of course, that know this. Some still teach the Albertus method of plant alchemy but they do not actually expect the student to obtain a quintessence from it because they know that is not possible. They teach it more as a method to get used to the mechanics of the glassware and for learning some vital processes, but what is obtained in the end is either a pile of goo or liquids that are not really a quintessence.

My argument with that is, why they cannot teach the valid lab processes in real plant work that results in something of substance? Either set of processes get students used to the glassware and such, except they could learn actual real alchemy at the same time. There is a way to do that.

The other way of looking at it comes from the path that corresponds with the same kind of work done in the mineral work. Doing pyrolytic (destructive) distillation of the plant materials, the same method used in the distillation of the Green Lion in the metallic work, will yield an entirely different set of materials; the philosophical Elements themselves.

This was brought to my attention by the modern alchemist Rubaphilos. The adept who wrote about this, well, there are several that wrote about it, but one that wrote about it very clearly was named Isaac Hollandus. Very clearly for an alchemist is not necessarily the same as reading it like *The Sunday Times*, but what he basically said was to take a substance and do a dry distillation and what one ends up getting are two primary things: A Red Fume and a White Fume. This is a nomenclature used by adepts who follow a path in alchemy that uses acetates as a step in their process. It is another way of saying one gets a Sulphur and a Mercury.

That way of presenting the philosophical Principals goes back to an older way of looking at alchemy where the binary nature of the process was more understood. However, before one can get either of those what one ends up getting is water, because even if the plant material is dry there is water in its structure. It takes a long time to drive out that water, close to ten hours because the heat cannot be cranked up or the right stuff is not obtained. It must be done slowly to drive out the moisture before increasing the temperature to get the other materials.

It was such a nuisance to the alchemists that some of them referred to it as the 'evil moisture' because they did not have electric hot plates. They could not just sit around, twiddling their thumbs and eating Cheetos while they were waiting and turning up the heat every 20 minutes. They had to keep the fire going, go get the wood and deal with a lot of potential problems. I can understand how they felt to a degree, even in this age, because driving out that moisture requires patience.

So one ends up with these three main liquids and the salt, which has to be purified out of the charred remains on the bottom of the flask. The volatile Salts which were mixed in with the fixed Salt in the Albertus method, are now in the liquid portion that Hollandus called the Red Fume.

The volatile Salt in the Hollandus process then gets separated out from the condensed Red Fume. In this viewpoint sometimes Mercury is called Water, and Sulphur is called Fire. When one understands that the Red Fume is also called Sulphur or Fire, and the volatile Salt that can be separated out of it can also be called an Earth, which is at that point still hidden in the Fire; when one reads 'Separate the Earth from Fire' in the *Emerald Tablet*, the meaning becomes clear. Very few practicing alchemists actually know what that phrase means, though they will often attempt to conceal that lack of understanding from others. There has only been one alchemist that ever explained it to me, and I know that other adepts know but they are not talking.

If that one thing had not been pointed out to me I may not have ever come to this kind of understanding. Granted, it is in Hollandus as well as other places, but it is very difficult to understand those texts unless someone has actually done, or at least seen, the process. Then one can read the text and see exactly what he means. Without the step of seeing, it would be a miracle to know that. Hollandus is a little more clear about a lot of things than some of the other adepts, even those who are writing about the same thing, but it is this process that leads closer to the things that are written and renowned in alchemy.

Of particular renown is the Mercury principal that becomes Philosophic Mercury. When this Mercury is distilled multiple times it behaves just like the legendary sources say of what Philosophic Mercury is supposed to do. It is called 'water that does not wet the hands.' It can be held in the palm of the hand. The problem is that it becomes volatile (evaporative) at really low temperatures, so one can hold it basically just long enough to watch it evaporate. It is a liquid and a water of sorts, and one's hand will not be wet. These are alchemical facts that were even mentioned in memoires about the Comte de Saint Germain, where he told Casanova that the liquid in the bottle he held was called *athoeter*, his name for Philosophic Mercury, and that if the wax seal were penetrated the liquid would evaporate. The Comte allowed him to do so, which proved that statement to be true.[7]

That is the universal plant Mercury, not ethanol or alcohol obtained from fermentation. Ethanol is a Mercury, to give it a label for discussion, because it does act as a solvent and it does do certain mercury-like things based on the philosophical Mercury idea; but that is not the real plant Mercury.

The reason why that is important is because of the other things true Philosophic Mercury does that allow one to obtain some substances along the path while working towards the Philosopher's Stone itself. Obtaining the Philosopher's Stone would of course be amazing, but honestly I am not focusing on the total completion of the Stone right now because I know that getting to true Philosophic Mercury is a whole lot closer, in a relativistic sense, than absolutely achieving the Philosopher's Stone. Philosophic Mercury allows one to obtain certain

---

[7] Hall, Manly P. "Introduction." In The Most Holy Trinosophia of the Comte De St.-Germain, XXII. 6th ed. Los Angeles, CA: Philosophical Research Society, 1983.

substances almost as prized as the Stone, that are renowned to do nearly the same things elixir-wise as can be obtained from the Stone, yet not being nearly as complex as the work towards the completed Stone itself. Additionally, those things of which I speak are required as components one needs to complete the Stone itself anyway, so there is little point in trying to get ahead of oneself. That is the beauty though, of having a solid working framework, a viable template, because through simple pragmatism it shows what is useful and productive, and what is essentially just premature distraction and non-productive use of time.

Those are distinctions my intuition was always telling me was not right about the Albertus plant path, but I could never quite put my finger on it. If it had not been brought to my attention, I know it would have taken longer to figure out. I might still be butting up against that wall. I would be making progress on the magical side but not so much in the alchemical side. It is important to understand that there is a very pivotal difference between the Albertus and Hollandus plant paths, and that has its own set of complications, but at least one knows one is on solid alchemical ground with Hollandus.

I did that process with my working group and we filmed it. We did not film the whole thing because it took 18 hours, but I wanted those I teach to be able to see the Red Fume and the White Fume for themselves—not just something I was talking about as an abstract, but literally see it. Seeing goes a long way to knowing. There is a 15-minute clip of that process on my website. One of the hurdles of that method is that it must be done more than once, and unlike the other work done in the beginning of the way I teach plant work where most of it can be done in the kitchen, the pyrolytic process should not be done inside.

I can say that from experience because I did it twice, because I just needed to do it. It took weeks to get the smell out of the house; it gets in everything. I should have known better because the alchemists referred to their Red Mercury as the 'stinking oil' because literally everything in the flask is burning.

Ever been around a house fire? That smell is very similar on a certain level and the last thing one needs is really mild smoke damage throughout the house. Spraying large amounts of essential oils all day long still took about three weeks to get that smell out of the house.

It should be done outside or in an environment built and designed to be able to do that, which is a more complex and expensive process one should work into after gaining some other experience. When I teach I do not start off with that process but I wanted everybody to see that process. It casts the light of illumination into the shadow areas present in modern plant alchemy.

Some will accept that light with a glad heart and move into a deeper level of understanding, while many will vehemently resist, especially those with vested financial interest in that game, because living into that knowledge with a pure heart will mean sacrificing what they have created upon the altar of Truth. I know that pain for myself because I created a brand of products, mostly incense and aromatics, that were very nicely packaged and presented. Over time it bothered me with increasing intensity that I had used the word 'alchemy' in the company name and in reference to herbs, incense, essential oils, and products that were not anywhere near to being quintessences. In and of themselves they had no right to be called alchemy. As my understanding and respect for true alchemy deepened I could no longer feel that using the word alchemy in those kinds of products lined up with my spiritual integrity. So I dismantled that brand. All of the money put into design and formulation, packaging, labeling, website design, advertising—I sacrificed all of that.

Even when I sold other things I personally owned and could have added that brand to the list, I retained it to ensure it stayed shut down. Once out of my hands I would not have had any control over it if I had let it go to anyone else. I could have sold it for good money and then walked away, but I would have still been responsible for yet one more thing existing in the world using the word alchemy in its name when it should not. That is how seriously I take the issue. Though I do not judge others if they do not do the same, I have made my sacrifices with a glad heart because real alchemy is far more important to me than a bunch of stuff that is not.

So my viewpoint of the problems about spagyrics and real alchemy, and the problems inherent in the status quo, have now been laid out pretty clearly, particularly when advanced herbal preparations are being sold as quintessences. *Caveat emptor!* If it is for sale and it is cheap, it is definitely not real quintessence.

The people that are doing that though, are not being disingenuous. They believe that what they have created is a true spagyric and some of them have had success in obtaining other alchemical essences. I have talked to some other alchemists and they have obtained some advanced alchemical Sulphurs, such as what is often called the 'oil of Mars' or the 'oil of Venus,' alchemical Sulphurs of iron and copper, respectively. Some of them have attained progress in stages of even more advanced mineral work, and because they were successful in those processes they believe that what they have created in their plant work is actually real—that those substances are really quintessences.

Somehow, it does not sink in that the experiences that they do have are not what they are supposed to be. The reason, with some of them, is that they are energetically sensitive. These are people that are really sensitively connected and they can feel really subtle differences through the filters of their own perceptions. They are perceiving the subtle differences between a regular extract and a really elaborate plant extract, not a quintessence: They are experiencing a slight subtle difference and to them that is validation that material is the substance that it is said to be.

Without the experience of knowing that an actual full strength quintessence can produce shocking effects, they do not have any way of making a real comparison. There is no, "I think I might feel something, wait, oh, well it could be..." No, there is none of that. They are serious things. They are serious, they are immediate, and they are profound; just like real magic. The reason seekers accept a mediocre substitute for alchemy is because they have accepted a mediocre substitute for magic as well. They just do not know that is what they have accepted.

Everybody has little experiences as they go along through their magical journey and those act as reinforcement, validating that they are on the right path. Those things are not accidents, those little things are placed there: They either tell us that we are on the right track or we are not, and they are not necessarily created to be helpful. There are intelligences whose job is to keep us separate until we have gained the right understanding to complete the rest of our journey.

Their job is to keep us in the box, basically, and when we get too close to the edges they find a way to close the box. If that means giving us this really trippy experience that we have been talking about for 20 years because that was the main thing that ever happened to us, then so be it. There is a lot of that.

One thing that I have learned from dealing with magical adepts and an alchemical adept is that they do not care about any of those stories. They will stop one half way through and say, "Blah, blah, blah, doesn't matter. Here's this work, do it. Write a report, tell me what happens." That is because they know the functions that are built in to keep seekers on a loop, to keep them busy, or distracted. That is not to invalidate the experiences themselves, because they are necessary, because without some of those experiences people would not continue on the path. They do serve a purpose, but it is not always as people think.

XIII

Traditional Viewpoint of Downplaying Plant Alchemy as Real Alchemy

The majority of those practicing modern lab alchemy have long held the idea that the Philosopher's Stone can only be made from the metallic kingdom. This is commonly accepted alchemical thought. In saying that the Philosopher's Stone can only be made from the metallic kingdom, they also assert that the beginning *prima* work with plants is only done to understand the processes and confect lesser Stones.

I prefer the path to quintessences that does not involve this plant Stone idea because every plant Stone I have ever seen made with the Albertus method basically looks like congealed snot. They are basically just balls of salt, essential oil, and alcohol congealed together until they make a really hard substance. People say they take them and get health benefits. I do not know anyone that has actually made a plant Stone from that Albertus method that actually can say that they had a profound quintessence experience.

They will say, "Oh, it tastes like rosemary, it is really intense or... blah, blah, blah." That is not why we make quintessence. For a really intense rosemary taste I can go to the store and buy rosemary extract and take a big swig. That is not why we do alchemy. I do not think that the majority of the 'Stones' that people make in the plant work are the slightest bit alchemical, because they are using the components from Albertus, not from Hollandus. If one is going to do it with Hollandus work, rock on. That is probably going to be a real plant Stone.

Of all the thousands of published manuscripts on alchemy there are only a handful that were explicit about plant work. The absence of plant work is conspicuous considering that it was the first work; it is the *prima* work yet there is little written about it. Many of the things that Paracelsus talked about that were plant related spoke to their virtues, or healing powers, but not really much to specific process.

Why is there is so little said about plant work in adept texts?

I think the adepts, those who knew real alchemy, understood that there are paths to the Philosopher's Stone through the vegetable kingdom that do not require having to do any of the metallic work. Hollandus pretty much plainly stated that as fact. When one thinks about how profound that is, it is tremendous, but it only makes sense if one has the philosophical Elements from the Hollandus plant work, and not the philosophical Principals from the Albertus plant work. That is also why long standing modern tradition does not jive with thinking plant alchemy is real alchemy; with these insights, their viewpoints are valid from a certain contextual angle.

I believe that the true adepts knew powerful quintessences could be made from the plant kingdom and they maintained their silence about it. There was no reason to fabricate fake texts for plant alchemy because of the commonly held idea that the real Stone was only metallic. There would not have been a market for plant texts, so there would not have been any reason for it on the side of either adepts or forgers. Adepts really went out of their way to not talk about it, considering it was the *prima* work.

The few plant work texts available, some of which are not popularly known, offer tremendous insight into the hidden potentials for working in alchemy without ever stepping outside the plant kingdom. I really like that because it allows one to focus productively without getting distracted into the realms that may not be fully productive to undertake without better understanding. The cool thing about making some progress in the plant work and obtaining quintessences is that when one ingests them one evolves not just physically, not just mentally, but with one's entire being: That means physically rejuvenative qualities depending on what is made, as well as rejuvenation of the mind.

Rejuvenation of the mind basically means correcting the dysfunctions that are in the lower mind. Quintessences allow access to higher states, to communicate more clearly with aspects of one's Higher Genius until it is possible to communicate with all things straight on, which is an important threshold, and then receive the guidance to the know how to work through the other kingdoms or paths. They are a conduit that gets one to the divine inspiration requirement, so even if one does not have a direct teacher, it is still a viable conduit to get to that divine inspired connection which really means some kind of connection with one's Higher Genius.

Deep progress in alchemy, and magic really requires that divine connection. That is one of the things that quintessences will help do. By learning to make them with the simplest of methods first, one can then work into the more advanced methods to obtain more powerful substances as proper knowledge and understanding allow. It gives time to get the body prepared to be able to deal with the higher levels of powerful spiritual medicines. It also facilitates understanding in a way that one could not do without them, unless one has a teacher giving exercises that then cause us to understand certain aspects about reality.

From my viewpoint real plant alchemy opens an entirely new and deeper level of green magic than most people probably ever really thought possible. With the proper keys to this practical work there is so much that can be explored when combined with other kinds of understanding. Generally, more magically focused work than anyone could ever really exhaust, but it is not just busy work. It is actually evolutionary busy work, so if one is not comfortable to step outside the plant path, I do not think it necessary. One may have to do more of something or less of something, to balance out the difference and the levels between plant work, mineral work, and work in the metallic kingdom, but not necessarily.

XIV

Higher Genii of Humans & Nature Intelligences

It is really important to understand what quintessences are and why they work. Part of that understanding is also understanding what humans are. This goes back to what used to be over the entrances of the ancient temples that held true, initiatory systems: Know Thyself.

'Know Thyself' does not mean knowing one's favorite color or any other personal likes and dislikes. What it means is knowing what one is ontologically, i.e. one's being: What is one's being made of in its parts, like the parts that we have talked about in the components obtained in lab work? Where do they come from? How do they come into form when one is born? Where do they go when one dies? What do they do while one is using them and when one is not using them? Where do they fit epistemologically in the greater whole of everything else? Those are really important concepts to understand about oneself in order to know one's place amongst all the other intelligences interacted with, consciously or unconsciously. Where those intelligences come from, and what their purpose is in addition to our own, are important concepts to understand to make any real progress in either alchemy or magic.

Entia means beings and in alchemy it is generally used in the term *Primum Ens*, meaning first being, or *Prima Entia*, first beings. It is talked about in the beginning often in relation to the

Primum Ens Melissae (the plant Melissa officinalis, which is Lemon Balm) because of what it does if it is a true quintessence. If it is just a tincture or an extract it is not going to do what the *Ens* does.

Prima Entia are the mother spirits of each species that exists within the Spirit of the World. Where humans have Higher Genii, the mother spirits are like the Higher Genius of the plant species, but not just the specific Melissa plant one is working on: All the Melissa plants everywhere that exist, ever have existed, or ever will exist have one mother spirit. That mother spirit is the nonphysical intelligence that rides in the physical vehicle that is created in the physical lab work. Think of it as constructing a chariot within which the mother spirit rides.

Alchemists are creating a physical thing that has a nonphysical component, and when that is ingested it creates a connection with the higher aspect of that intelligence that resides within the Spirit of the World. That opens the alchemist to whatever powers are conveyed by that particular essence universally because humans are a simulacrum of everything that exists in the entirety of creation, in a certain way.

That means that everything that exists archetypally in the universe exists within humans in an embryonic form. It is not that one just already has it and just needs to remember, which is just one concept amongst a number of popular new age half truths. One does have them but only in an embryonic state, and by taking certain quintessences and doing some certain work one can cause them to grow. As they grow, one's consciousness shifts. One then experiences reality in a different way. There are all kinds of things that happen as a result of ingesting Higher Genii from different kingdoms. It is like eating evocation.

That is the way I explain it. It has never really been said exactly that way to me, though perhaps something close, but because my personal focus is very magical, in theory and in research, I have a certain way of looking at things. That is the way I present it because it is the way that makes sense to me.

XV

Prima Entia vs. Other Plant Work

In plant alchemy one works towards obtaining the *Primum Ens* of a plant, a quintessence, which is a particular class of substance. A plant Stone, if it is a Stone made truly and properly, should be a quintessence, but there is another process for obtaining quintessence. There is a lot of work still required but it is not nearly as much work as making a Stone.

Number one, if one has to go through 18 hours of distillation to get little portions of philosophical Principals to get enough of the right materials to make a Stone, then just that part of the process is far more complex, though infinitely instructive. With the *Ens* process, which is what alchemists have come to call it, it is a way to obtain plant quintessences without having to go through pyrolytic distillation. The only obstacle there really is in that process is the use of alcohol, for people that have alcohol addiction issues.

If someone is an alcoholic the traditional *Ens* process is the last thing that one can safely handle. It is not just that one has to use something with alcohol, it must be absolutely dry alcohol. It must be absolutely dry of water which means 200 proof. That is a bit of an obstacle. There is a way to deal with it, but for some it is a real obstacle.

In the *Ens* process use of alcohol is okay because one is not obtaining quintessence in the same way. It is an entirely different process and basically, one is using the alcohol as a solvent medium to allow the *Ens* to transfer from a saturated solution of salts into an ingestible substance. The alcohol and salts are binaries of each other, which means they repel each other in a certain way. When one does that process one is obtaining the *Ens* within the alcohol portion, which is then siphoned off, and concentrated down to obtain pure *Ens*, or at least a saturated solution of *Ens* to make handling it more practical.

The cool thing is, that in place of the alcohol which is usually used as the solvent material, this does not have to be an alcohol technically. The philosophic Mercury (the White Fume, the White Wine) from the Hollandus process, the basis of what later becomes the Philosophic Mercury, can be used in place of the ethanol portion of the traditional *Ens* process, because it too is a binary of the salts and it is ingestible. So for someone that wants to pursue this, and is dedicated enough to deal with all that is necessary in the Hollandus method to get that single material, one can still do plant alchemy and participate in the *Ens* method. In certain alchemical texts this liquid from the White Fume, 'the water that does not wet the hands,' is often called Acetone, but again that is a philosophical name. It is not like the acetone in the hardware store, it is just called Acetone. Just like the spirit of wine is called Mercury and the other things called Sulphur but contain no actual elemental sulphur.

Philosophic Principals were named those things because of the qualities those things have, like elemental mercury being liquid but being metal, which is unique and very symbolic. Elemental sulphur also has interesting properties and it was those behaviors that inspired alchemists to name their philosophical Sulphur after it.

Elemental mercury may in other traditions be the starting material for creating quintessence. I do not have specific reason to doubt it, I just do not trust most of what is written about it and I do not know anyone reliable enough to teach me otherwise. Maybe that will change. That would be cool, mostly out of curiosity, but also unnecessary because I know that the path and lineage that I am following is a proper alchemical path and I prefer to focus on something of known productivity before indulging in other speculative endeavors, no matter how interesting they may be.

Ingestion of the *Ens* begins an integration of the alchemist's consciousness with the Higher Genius of the plant and affects consciousness. The reason Melissa is started with is because it is renowned in alchemy as a rejuvenative. One of the challenges that alchemists have always had in the Great Work is living long enough to complete the Great Work. Death is a threshold placed there on purpose for lots of reasons but it is something that has to be thought about. What kicked my butt into gear was a teacher I know, who basically said any alchemist worth his Salt starts creating a rejuvenative as soon as he is able to do it.

Instead of four or five years of busy work with all that Albertus plant work hoo-ha that I understand and do not agree with, it is better to start out working on the *Ens* process. It is simple but it is not easy. For the most part the mechanics of it, if one comes to understand how the philosophical Principals work, one can figure out more than one way to get the *Ens*. For example, using the philosophical Acetone (White Fume) obtained in Hollandus work to replace the ethanol used in *Ens* work. No one ever told me that, I just figured it out one day while studying various texts and deeply contemplating the *Ens* process.

That is absolutely not the way it is normally taught, but of the handful of references to making *Ens*, none of them are the same.

I am not convinced that all of them even lead to an *Ens*. Descriptions of processes are not overly explicit in their instructions, which is not to say they are incomplete. In comparing some of them though, they do not all line up. Even in the writings of Paracelsus who wrote copiously, there is one single paragraph about the *Ens*:

"Take celandine or balm; beat them into a pulse, shut them up in a glass vessel Hermetically sealed, and place in horse dung to be digested a month. Afterwards separate the pure from the impure, pour the pure into a glass vessel with dissolved salt, and let this, when closed, be exposed to the sun for a month. When this period has elapsed, you will find in the bottom a thick liquid, and the salt floating on the surface. When this is separated you will have the virtues of the balm or of the celandine, as they are in their first entity, and these are called, and really are, the first entities of balm or of the celandine."[8]

That is it, so again, the information is conspicuous by its relative absence. Doing this work requires diligent trial and error, to a degree. It is not that one does not know what one is doing in theory, but getting the ratios right takes practice. The above method is not the method I personally use to obtain *Ens* because there are much more efficient methods to use, though that is a method that bypasses the use of alcohol as a menstruum.

The way it is normally taught is having the pure alcohol and having what are called deliquesced plant salts. Potassium carbonate is hygroscopic, it just sucks up water. Traditionally deliquescing was done by putting out sheets of glass in a cellar

---

[8] The Great, Paracelsus. "The Book Concerning Renovation and Restoration, The First Entity of Herbs." In The Hermetic and Alchemical Writings of Paracelsus, edited by Arthur E. Waite, 135. Vol. II. Mansfield Centre, CT: Martino Publishing, 209.

because cellars were damp, and spreading out potassium carbonate on them, and then collecting liquid off of it. Some put it in containers outside at night to get moisture from the dew. This has led to various notions of alchemists collecting starlight, and moonlight, and all kinds of 'energies' and that has nothing to do with it. It just needs to be a saturated solution of plant salt and that is how they did it because it was easier for them at that time.

They also did not have pollutants like today. 500 years ago, when they said, "Just put your plant salts outside and they will deliquesce," and they did not have to worry about acid rain and all kinds of stuff in the environment that I do not need in my salts. I learned how to create saturated solution of potassium carbonate in the kitchen with distilled water because I am not collecting moonlight and starlight.

The other thing that led me to do this in the kitchen was that by the time I got around to trying to collect it, even though I lived in a very humid environment, that was the one week there was no humidity. I woke up at 6:00 in the morning to go outside and collect casserole pans of deliquesced plant salts and there was not any. I am not a morning person so that was not going to work for me. After six days of that I was like, "You know what, I am over this particular collection method. It is just not going to happen."

But people really do believe because it has been continually taught and promoted so, that it is energy from the stars one is collecting, but that goes back to adding something extra that is not needed. There is nothing wrong with energy from the stars, there is energy from the stars; it is called radiation. We live in the sea of it, but that is not vital to the process of creating a quintessence.

XVI

Entheogens & Prima Entia

Entheogens are plants, such as ayahuasca or peyote, that often have long standing traditional use in shamanic practices. They can also be things like *Amanita* mushrooms or *Salvia divinorum*, which is said to have been Gandhi's favorite herb.

According to the online *Oxford English Dictionary*, an entheogen is **"A psychoactive substance which is used in a religious ritual or to bring about a spiritual experience, typically a plant or fungal extract; (more widely) any hallucinogenic drug."**

While the Oxford definition describes how they may be used to seek a 'spiritual experience' it does not elaborate further. Entheogen only made its appearance in the dictionary as a word in 1979.

My general working definition of an entheogen is: **A plant that has strong concentrations of alkaloids, which when ingested have receptors in the brain that allow people to open up to certain aspects of God, or alternative levels of reality.**

To make full disclosure here, I have never actually taken these substances. I have never really taken drugs or anything to alter my consciousness through a chemical means in that way. It is not because I have any moralistic objections, because I do not, but rather because weird enough things were already happening to me. I wanted to make sure that my experiences were in no way drug induced, that they were happening on a true psychospiritual level.

I did take ecstasy one time, because I wanted to see what all the fuss was about. And I get it, but I do not need to do it again. I see why people take it. My experience was not that it was that much different than really, really deep, intense meditation where one is open to everything; only, it takes all of ten minutes. Coming down off it is not fun, and that is the part I am not interested in repeating.

The reason I talk about entheogens is because it really ties into understanding the ideas of the Higher Genii of plants. With *Salvia divinorum*, for example, when people take it, it is very common that two reactions occur.

Statistically speaking, there are a lot of published accounts of what happens. Either, people have a horrible experience, and come away from it saying, "Oh, that was awful, I never want to do that again." Or, often they have an experience where they can end up meeting the children in a more pleasant way, which is the way the intelligence often presents itself to the people that have taken it.

My thoughts on that are that many of the people that are taking these substances and having bad experiences are simply trying to trip. They are abusing them because they just want another way to take a drug to escape their lives and entheogens are something they can get a hold of and try. That approach to the plants is disrespectful.

They may not be doing that on purpose, but the plant spirits do not really care. Doing it for anything other than a pure reason, to have a spiritual experience, warrants them giving one that ensures not wanting to come back. All of the spirits are capable of doing that, but the ones that are from plants called entheogens are particularly noted for doing that, probably because they are the ones that have the alkaloids that allow people to access them simply though a chemical gateway.

Humans have receptors for those alkaloids that open awareness up to certain levels that are normally blocked from the conscious mind: Then plant spirits have access to directly communicate.

Proper approach to entheogens can have profound effects. Ayahuasca is part of a longstanding spiritual tradition, and used properly, prepared properly, and ingested properly, has been well documented to lead people to profound spiritual depths and a better understanding of themselves, the world around them, and the interconnectedness of everything.

The main difference between using an entheogen versus ingesting *Ens* over a period of time is quite distinct. Ingesting the *Ens*, thereby integrating the mother spirit into consciousness, is more gradual but can also be more permanent, whereas the entheogens process out of the system pretty quickly, and then that connection is closed. There is no permanent connection forged, though if someone were actually magically trained in the proper technique to constructively negotiate with the mother spirit of the plants that are used as entheogens, then they could perhaps maintain a more permanent contact.

The difficulty with that kind of permanent integration is that many of the entheogens are also moderately to extremely hallucinogenic, so it may also be that maintaining a more permanent connection with them could be more interruptive to normal consciousness than beneficial. It is very difficult to maintain a normal thinking consciousness, and grounded decision making, as those things are not really part of entheogen use due to their hallucinogenic nature. That is just not how that class of plants generally works. It is a limitation; possibly a limitation created on purpose because it does make one dependent upon the plant to access certain abilities.

Shamans that use the plant to be able to journey into other levels of reality and do their healing work, become dependent upon the plant. Whereas, with the alchemists point of view, though in the specific case of entheogens it may not apply, ingesting the *Ens* until a more permanent connection is made where one is no longer dependent upon ingesting the *Ens* of that particular plant is a more permanent goal.

The *Ens* is not physical. The *Ens* itself, the mother spirit, is nonphysical. When doing practical work alchemists create the physical structure for the quintessence, like a physical chariot for that nonphysical intelligence, to ride in. It gives it a vehicle within physical substance that when ingested lets go of the physical vehicle and then that intelligence integrates with consciousness.

It is not that the quintessences are not physical because they have a physical component, but the *Ens* itself is nonphysical. That is a very important thing to remember in this whole process. That is why there are similar aspects between entheogens and the *Ens*, but real alchemists do not do these things to just trip. There is enough trippy stuff in magic and alchemy on the real level, when one becomes ripe enough, one does not need to go looking for it. At a certain point things just happen.

A major point of alchemical distinction is that the powers of the *Ens* of a particular plant do not necessarily correlate with the known effects of the plant as it is used in herbalism or shamanism, because the quintessence itself is something that physically did not exist before its creation. Alchemists take separated substances and make One Thing out of those components; a new state of being that did not previously exist.

One of the challenges the alchemical community has as a group, and one of the reasons why I wanted to put a private group together in the first place is that there is extremely limited information on *Prima Entia*. The more people are part of a working group the more individual research can be done across a wider range of species.

One alchemist can only do so much research on so many plants. Because it is not just making the *Ens*, it has to be ingested for a while to see what the effect of a particular Ens is. The rejuvenative effects of Melissa and a couple of the other plants are known because they have been handed down.

There are only five plants that are known as to what they do as *Entia* and they all basically are rejuvenatives. Those are the ones that were passed down. I am of the opinion that while most quintessences are probably rejuvenative to some extent, that plants store other aspects of the archetypal forces that can be integrated through plant work if more is learned about what specific plant species do at the *Ens* level.

It may be a bit ambitious to set a crazy goal of thousands to figure out, but I think a group of a decent size can certainly come to terms with more than five. I do not think that is a stretch. I may be wrong; it may be that other *Entia* of plants do not have as much effect as the traditional five that are classed as rejuvenatives, though I have had considerable experience now from my own work with the *Ens* of Oak. Until more work is done across a wider spectrum it is impossible to say with certainty, but my own work thus far seems to be fleshing out my working hypothesis as being correct.

Another issue with the traditional information is the length of time the *Ens* was taken. When people take the *Primum Ens Melissae*, with all the stories about it, people take it for a little while and then they stop, with no clear explanation. Some of them probably stop because of some of the stories that are renowned about it, which once they see happening for themselves, cause them to abandon their course.

One of the things the *Primum Ens Melissae* does as a rejuvenative is push out all of the toxins that are not supposed to be in the body. It purifies. It does not heal disease or other conditions that are already fully manifested, but it will purify out toxins. That means pushing out things that are taking up residence in the body like fungal infections and things like that. So most of the stories about these old guys that took the *Ens*, and then documented what happened, said their fingernails and toenails fell out.

In those cases there was likely not any actual toenail left, it was just probably fungus, which is why it fell out. It is not that perfectly good stuff is going to fall out. It is also known that dental fillings are renowned for coming out during this process. Some people have a real problem with that. I was emailing with one of the alchemists in Saudi Arabia telling him feedback from some of the people that I talked to where they were all gung-ho to do *Ens* work. Then when they found out their dental fillings might fall out they were terrified because of the mercury in them, which then sets up a fear that stops the work.

The alchemist said, "That is irrational, because if it is purifying you, it is pushing out the stuff that is not supposed to be there, which includes the mercury." To which I replied, "Yes, I know that. But, people do not usually make decisions using logic, they make them based on emotion most of the time, and if they get caught up in fear, they are definitely not making them on logic." So this has been a thing where people say, "Yes, I want to do alchemy; yes, I want to take quintessences; yes, I want to be transformed; but no, I do not want anything to change."

That is not going to happen. Either alchemy is real or it is not. That is another reason people have been content to play with advanced herbalism and call it alchemy, because then they do not really have to change but still get the emotional satisfaction of tinkering with glassware. Personally I would rather just go hang out on the beach. I do not need to make a really elaborate diversion for myself if I am not actually going to get anything practical out of it.

There are things that happen as a result of ingesting true quintessence. If there are extreme dysfunctions in the mind they get purified too. If one's life is structured around those dysfunctions and all the sudden things are being brought into alignment, and one no longer relates to those dysfunctions, things in that person's life are going to fall away. That may be extremely painful. One may have a dysfunctional relationship: People become terrified that, "Oh, I might not have my relationship" or "I might not this, or I might not have that" and they stop. That is what fear does. It stops one from evolving.

It is not that these are not legitimate, rational concerns or feelings. It is just either someone really wants substantial spiritual growth and is going to buck up and take the medicine and deal with changes, whatever they look like, or one is not really, truly looking for that.

Even if somebody is not, it is okay. This information gets planted as a seed in consciousness. Maybe this lifetime one is not going to do it, but maybe next time will. If the seed does not ever get planted nothing can grow. So I do not have an attachment to whether a specific person does it or not. In fact, most of the time I try to discourage people who are not absolutely serious from doing it because I know how much work it is, which is a waste if one does not follow through all the way. I also know the work is worth it, to be able to learn anything real about alchemy. Applying it to the plant kingdom to obtain quintessence that allows one to forge a connection with *Prima Entia* to expand one's spiritual consciousness is an amazing thing!

Prima Entia rule their species, but also hold powers related to specific aspects of natural laws. Every plant does something different on a spiritual level and has a reason for existing.

On every level everything that exists archetypally, also exists on every other level, which means all the universal powers that exist theoretically should exist in the plant kingdom somewhere, in the same way that they all exist within humans embryonically. I believe that it is only finding them and identifying them, much like the specific quests shamans undertake to find and acquire plant spirits, though the purpose and way in which they are used differ.

So there is a lot of research to be done on that front, which is really cool because it is a lot more accessible for most people to do this work, than it is to do the more advanced processes. Yet, this is still actually real alchemy, because real quintessences are obtained. As opposed to five years of screwing around with the Albertus *prima* work as it is normally taught just to learn the mechanics of glassware and some philosophical concepts. Those are indeed important, but, one can learn those lessons by doing something real. At least with *Ens* work one is making progress in the actual 'doing' of real alchemy.

XVII

Quintessences as Rewards on the Path to the Stone

Advanced alchemy is an unique puzzle. There are many stages and processes, but if one is following a real path, the unique materials obtained are not only usually prerequisites for getting to the next level, but sometimes are known to have incredible benefits in and of themselves, like creating the potables: Specifically Potable Gold, and Potable Silver, once Philosophic Mercury is obtained.

What is really groovy about the advanced work with pyrolytic distillation is attaining the White Fume or the philosophical Mercury portion from which the Philosophic Mercury is created. One learns to make Philosophic Mercury from that White Fume, which involves a certain process of taking up into it other specific materials that have been obtained and purified. They have to be taken up into the Mercury in a certain sequence, kind of like a three-dimensional puzzle, or they will not all get in there.

So the order must be known, the sequence that it is taken up in, but once one succeeds in obtaining that, then all that is needed to obtain Potable Gold is to take elemental gold and put it in there. What Philosophic Mercury does is separate things (called radical dissolution) into philosophical Principals all by itself, at ambient temperature. Just put it in there and that is what it does, which is a very cool thing. So Potable Gold and Silver are basically the philosophical Sulphur portions, the soul portions, of physical gold and physical silver. The body and spirit are also separated out, but the soul portions, the philosophical Sulphurs, are the potable essences being sought. The are often called the 'Oil of Gold', or 'Oil of Silver,' and they are required as ferments in later production of the Philosopher's Stone itself—but, as rewards along the path, they also convey benefits to the alchemist when ingested.

Now, metals do not have 'oils' even though tradition refers to them as such, but everything natural that exists has a philosophical Sulphur principal, and the Philosophic Mercury separates it out. So, Potable Gold, and Potable Silver are rewards on the path that are ingestible and which heal in many ways.

Potable Silver cures mental things and issues with the nervous system. Potable Gold is renowned to be almost as effective as the Elixir of Life, but far easier to obtain, theoretically, when talking about the complexity of making the Philosopher's Stone, which cannot even begin until achieving success in making the Philosophic Mercury. The Stone is a much more complex level of work.

As alchemists work towards completing the Philosopher's Stone, they have to create other things to be able to do that work, but as they succeed in creating those things they get rewards. Those rewards let them live longer and be healthier in order to have more time to complete the Great Work.

So it is not that one makes a plant quintessence and gets to live a really long time. One can maintain a certain biological age for a period of time, but is still going to have to work towards Philosophic Mercury if one wants to really be able to cure disease out of the body. The *Primum Ens Melissae* will purify, but it is not necessarily going to purge specific conditions that have already started to take form within the body.

The ultimate level is the actual Philosopher's Stone, from which one is able to make the Elixir of Life, which is basically just taking tiny portions of the Stone and putting it in something ingestible to drink. It is the dosage that is the issue.

With Potable Gold and Potable Silver, the dosages are still an issue, but it is not as much of an issue because they are just the separated philosophical Sulphurs: They are not physical God in a Stone.

The complexity after first attaining the Stone is still quite considerable. Obtaining it is one thing. Multiplying it and increasing its power is a whole other process. It is very similar to the first part of that stage, but it is still not easy to do that work. At any point along the way it can get screwed up, and then there is nothing to do but start over. Of course, one will get there faster because of having done it before. That is part of the heartache that a lot of alchemists have gone through. They have succeeded in obtaining the Stone, but then not necessarily knowing how it is multiplied, or any of the other details. At a certain point they were on their own, left to trial and error, and the best that they could deduce through their own consciousness, if they had contact with anything that was helping them, or anything that adepts wrote on the subject. There is not a lot of information written about that part. It is just not talked about. The working assumption is if one can get that far, then one can figure the rest out. It does not mean it is going to happen the first time.

XVIII

Understanding Allegory— Its Purpose & Misdirection

According to the online *Oxford English Dictionary*, 'allegory' is defined as: **"A story, poem, or picture that can be interpreted to reveal a hidden meaning, typically a moral or political one."**

For spiritual seekers I do not find this definition to be helpful because if one could just easily and accurately interpret the allegory to reveal its hidden meaning, it would not really be hidden. The conclusions most often arrived at from this sort of thinking are generally not accurate, thus the allegory has done its job.

My working definition of allegory is a bit more distilled, but rather cuts to the point of how it is used in alchemy, magic, and religion in general: **"Truth wrapped in clever lies. It is never what it looks like."**

Alchemists use a lot of allegory, and there is a ton of allegory in religion. It is there for a reason.

Passing along the understanding of something, is not as effective as passing on along the allegory, because allegory is easier to pass. If someone gains understanding then one can see the allegory for what it is, but if one does not have the proper understanding, one is just going to believe the allegory in either a literal or a symbolic way, which is most of what religion is.

That does not invalidate religion itself; it is still talking about very real things: They are just not what their adherents believe they are. They have been lead to their conclusions on purpose, in a manner of misdirection. The thing is, if it is true on one level, it has to be true on all levels. However, the knowledge of how that truth is applied on each level is usually very different and definitely not obvious. So that is the challenge of figuring out allegory.

So, an example is, the conjunction of the Sun and the Moon as principal alchemical allegory. This is advanced work, and it relates to both inner and physical work, but it is mostly talked about in inner work—which is odd because adepts do not talk about inner work very much. It is often only seen in depictions of processes.

In this allegory the Sun and Moon are depicted as male and female, but really it relates to the conscious and unconscious mind. So the enactment of allegory in ritual and ceremonial within religion was meant as a vehicle for preserving the allegory; however, the enactment of the allegory is not the process itself.

So in magical practice, it is used symbolically in ritual to affect the psyche, the entire complex: Although that can work under proper instruction, that is the part most often missing. The most common application of this allegory is an attempt to use physical sex as a magical process, which does not really work very well. Polarity shift can happen, though it is very rare. One problem is, that it does not usually work when it is contrived on the physical level through the use of ritual.

Aleister Crowley is a case in point. He spent years bouncing back and forth between male and female companions, for the specific purpose of messing with his polarity—trying to make the conjunction of the Sun and the Moon happen. I am not convinced that he ever did. The only reason I have that opinion is because that happened to me a long time ago, and I was not trying to do it on purpose.

My only purpose was taking myself out of a certain box that I felt no longer served my highest good. Freeing myself from self-imposed limitation was my objective, but I did not even think about it in the context of anything else. And when that conjunction happened, I was absolutely astounded, because it was not, "Oh, I think I felt something." It was like the left side of my body slammed into the right, and the right slammed into the left, and I knew exactly what happened. It was the most peculiar thing. Having the experience was one thing, coming to understand it has been a long and winding process.

So, since the autumn of 1997, that is the way I have been inside. So I am in a male body, but I do not necessarily know that I feel one way or the other. It is just the way it is.

That shift was brought about as a culmination between past magical work, and consciousness development through magical practice and meditation, but the actual happening itself had absolutely nothing to do with what I was doing during the moments that it occurred. It seemed more to do with willingness and surrender, which was definitely a factor, but in the end it was predominantly a ripeness issue.

When consciousness is ripe enough for certain things to happen, they happen. Just like when an apple is ripe enough to fall off a tree, it is going to happen. It does not matter how much one prays to keep an apple on a tree, it is going to fall.

So, when I say that I do not think Crowley succeeded, it is because in the writings that he left, most of the time, he was really kind of ambiguous about that particular subject, mostly because he was trying to figure it out, so there was not 100% clarity as to whether it actually worked or not. He believed in the process of the polarity changing, but his attempts were contrived, on the errant notion that his lower will could somehow be forced upon the higher.

I have lots of thoughts on Crowley, though his Thelemites do not particularly like all of them. I think he was very cool in spite of having extreme egotism. I think that he was, for his time, quite amazing. He survived the Victorian era, and being mentally tortured as a child because his father was a strict, fundamentalist minister. I think for who he was and what he had to work with, and the fact that he did not actually have initiation from an adept, regardless of who gave him a ceremony, and whatever fancy title was held. He and his predecessors were revivalists trying to figure things out. They did make headway in some areas, but they were not real adepts. Not according to the definitions I use, which are the definitions of the adepts under which I studied. They just do not line up with those definitions. The well-documented history of infighting and backstabbing amongst themselves simply serves to further illustrate the point.

It does not diminish what Crowley accomplished as a person. It just means that he started off with a severe handicap, and made it through a lot of interesting experiences. As a result of that, though, in combination with the general mindset of the Victorian era, mixed with Freudian and Jungian thought, and all of the things that came about in that time, led to some of the bizarre notions that Crowley derived; mainly some really inaccurate notions about sex and magic, and teaching that those things are somehow alchemy when they are not. They are not at all alchemy.

I do not care how many magic triangles someone draws in the air, that is not alchemy. Or, whether one calls sex on an altar the 'Great Rite' and says that is alchemy. And, I do not care how many times someone sticks a blade into a chalice and stirs wine to call it consecrated, that is not alchemy. It is allegory, and there is a ton of it.

And it is all useful, because, allegory is very easy to pass along though religion. The danger is that people believe it literally instead of trying to understand it even metaphorically. Some people do take things metaphorically and that is at least a step up from literal.

Understanding it allegorically though is a step up from metaphor. That is when one understands that it really has absolutely nothing to do with what can be seen, in terms of the ritual itself. In the example of the blade and chalice, the allegory is about learning how to make the male and female aspects of the psyche become One Thing.

That is the beauty of allegory as well as the danger of it, because in order to preserve allegory, Mystery Traditions are created which later end up spawning religions that eventually devolve into crazy and hopelessly inaccurate understandings of complex esoteric ideas.

XIX

Allegory in Practical Lab Work

Considering this idea of the Sun and Moon, and taking the allegory into practical lab work, it is necessary to unravel the Sun and the Moon naming conventions, which requires understanding what those substances are on an alchemical level. The common awareness in the magical community of the Sun being Fire and the Moon being Water is only a surface level idea.

To get anywhere in real alchemy, one must understand how these Elements really line up, in terms of the different ways that they are presented: Sun, Fire, Sulphur, Red Fume; Moon, Water, Mercury, White Fume. These are all different ways in certain aspects of practical laboratory work of saying the exact same things. Or, describing perhaps different levels of the same work, in slightly different processes, but this is always what adepts refer to in some manner or another.

It can get more than a little confusing, which is why when reading an adept it is necessary to stay holistically within the document he created. Jumping between documents before accurate understanding will only lead in circles. Once these different conventions are known and understood, they become easier to interpret: Lully called these things Red Wine and White Wine; other adepts called them Red Mercury and White Mercury; Hollandus called them Red Fume and White Fume; and others yet called them simply Sulphur and Mercury.

Raymond Lully is considered to be the founding adept that wrote about this particular process within the tradition of Western alchemy, which some now call the acetate path because of how work is done on the advanced mineral level. Lully (ca. 1235-1315 C.E.) and Hollandus (ca. 1572-1610 C.E.) are clearly involved in the same tradition, but over time, each referred to the philosophical Elements in slightly different ways. It may have been done on purpose to a certain extent, because they were aware of the fact that over one long span of time, alchemists refer to the same thing by many different names. So if they had all called it Red Wine and White Wine, it would have been an obvious tie that those things were connected, but they had the wisdom in that age to do otherwise.

These men were more clever than can ever be comprehended, even in the way that they just had to live and work. These were people that could probably just work a cryptex because that was just part of daily life when one was an alchemist in the Medieval age.

Experiencing the process these adepts taught, rather than just trying to understand it intellectually, helps instill a better way to relate to this aspect of Nature. Even just seeing it one time begins to illuminate what the adepts wrote, even though they did not say everything. It gives a solid starting point to practical understanding.

I created a post on my blog with a video for those who would like to see the first stage of that process:

https://www.transcendenceworks.com/videos/

XX

Unveiling Alchemical Allegory in Religion

The crux of allegory is to take something and spin it into something else, like the idea behind the Language of the Birds, also known as the Green Language, or *Lingua Verdi*, of the alchemists, which was a 'language' Saint Francis of Assisi was purported to understand. In the imagery of Saint Francis, he is usually surrounded by birds and animals, and the popular Catholic notion is that he could speak to them. Though he may have developed the ability to do that, that is not the meaning behind those alchemical ideas.

The Saint Francis story endures precisely because it is allegory, not because of what people thought the allegory meant.

One level of the Language of the Birds was a clever way of using words in one language that sound like words in other languages, the one word concealing the nature of the meaning conveyed by the other. Just reading something written in Green Language would yield the reader little fruit if knowledge of this fact were unknown, particularly since one of the main languages employed in this manner, particularly by French adepts, was archaic Greek.

Another level of the Language of the Birds has to do with an adept's ability to find the true and deepest meanings inherent in symbols as living intelligences, by communicating with them

113

directly as aspects of universal mind.

To take the idea of unveiling allegory in religion into a deeper and more complex idea, one has only to turn to the core teaching allegory within Christianity.

That allegory is, "Except a man be born again, he cannot see the kingdom of God."[9]

The problem is in understanding what 'born again' actually means, from an adept alchemical point of view. Alchemists understand that in addition to a physical body, humans have a solar body and a lunar body, which is another way of saying humans have a spirit and a soul. In order to be 'born' into the stellar body, the glorified body of light, the sun and the moon have to completely conjoin with the physical body; just the same as in the lab work where the alchemist must get the philosophical Sulphur, Mercury, and Salt to become One Thing.

That is being 'born again' because one ends up with a new body. One cannot get to Heaven until achieving that body, because one does not exist in the right configuration to access that level of existence.

Everyone is meant to evolve to attain that body of light. How long it takes is relative to each individual's spiritual evolution. What Christ said means exactly that. What people do not realize is that the kingdom of Heaven is a state of consciousness.

"The kingdom is inside you and it is outside you."[10]

---

[9] John 3:3 King James Version

[10] Meyer, Marvin, and Harold Bloom. "Saying 3." In The Gospel of Thomas: The Hidden Sayings of Jesus, 23. First ed. New York, NY: HarperCollins Publishers, 1992.

Heaven is not a place, it is a state of consciousness that once attained allows one to access multiple levels of reality: "In my Father's house are many mansions."[11]

Heaven is the state of eternity, no time, and no physical limitation because one has become the Stone, or in esoteric Christian terms attained the Robe of Glory, which is in perfect alignment with the *Emerald Tablet* where it says, "Thus will you obtain the Glory of the whole Universe. All obscurity will be clear to you. This is the greatest force of all powers, because it overcomes every Subtle thing and penetrates every Solid thing." It corresponds in Qabala to the state of *Binah*, called Understanding, which is a conjunction in Hebrew of *Ben Yah*, which means 'Sons of God.'

Thus, one cannot enter the kingdom of Heaven unless one becomes a Son of God.

Accurately unraveling that allegory leads to understanding the alchemy behind the mechanics of how things work on a higher epistemological and ontological basis. Some of the teachings will overlap, because bits and pieces are left in the magical tradition, in the alchemical tradition, and pieces are in religious writings. Figuring out how to line up the pieces in a way that reveals how things work unlocks those doors.

Humans come back, evolve, die, get reborn, evolve some more, and keep doing it until they get ripe enough as spiritual fruit that the Higher Genii can harvest them, and say, "Okay. You do not have to do that any longer. You are now going to evolve into the next level of being."

We come back here and we do this over and over and over

---

[11] John 14:2 King James Version

again, and we struggle. People that want to run around and pretend that they are victims to the process do not really understand that it is not being done to abuse us, and it is not being done for anything other than that is how we evolve to the next level of being. It is absolutely necessary, and somebody cannot come along and do it vicariously for us. That cannot happen.

Looking at nature, there are many examples of what happens when someone messes with it. Just watch a butterfly break out of its cocoon: It struggles, and it struggles, and it struggles, and if one has any empathy at all, the impulse is to help it; but the problem is that if it does not force, if it does not struggle, if it does not push against that cocoon, it does not develop the muscles needed to fly. So, one could help it get out of the cocoon, but it is going to die because it cannot fly.

We are no different in our metamorphoses, as chrysalides, in this process. It requires more incarnations, and it is more complicated, but it is the same process. So, the idea of vicarious atonement only goes so far. It is not that there is not a Christ aspect, because there is: It is an aspect of one's Higher Genius on a personal level.

Humans can attain to that personal threshold when they reach a level of Solar consciousness; *Tiphereth* in Qabala is directly related to that Solar consciousness. Humans can learn to communicate with that aspect if they are taught the right technique. I can attest that is absolutely a true statement because I was taught that process. It is a core part of the process one learns if receiving correct instruction within the true Western Mysteries.

What the Western Mystery Tradition always provided between the Lesser Mysteries, which are lunar, and the Greater

Mysteries, which are solar, were all of the key pieces that go together. Those keys expose one to forces that one has to evolve through in order to create that next state of consciousness: To step across the Abyss and reach the state of becoming a Son of God.

Humans have that embryonically on one level but it is not a level they have access to experience directly without training and development. That level IS the Higher Genius. Technically, the Higher Genius is eternal. One can fool around with this for lifetimes, it does not really care on a certain scale, but it is the one pulling the strings, it is the one creating one's experiences.

It is continually molding reality to shape one into becoming what it wants one to become. That is why it is wrong to hold judgment of what other people do, whether it is felt to be personally egregious or not. Ultimately until humans reach a state of consciousness where they are allowed to have the reins, which is that state of consciousness of being Sons of God, they are not really, fully, totally in control.

Basically, to a certain extent humans are sock puppets. We are not in control of anything. We try, we still have to do our best, but really, the Higher Genii are in control. So, on one hand that is kind of liberating, and on the other hand, it feels a little weird.

The whole point of getting to a certain state of conscious is so that one can fully merge with the Higher Genius and then have reached that level of evolution. All the other stages in between are just simply steps on the ladder that have to be climbed, and each one of them is a little weird and different, and often contrary to intuition because those obstacles are put there by Nature to keep things from going where they are not ready to go.

Everything important has a Guardian. If one is not supposed to go there, its job is to keep one out. As soon as one evolves to the point where one is supposed to be there, that Guardian no longer blocks access and can often function as a preliminary guide, but it is the same intelligence. Guardians have a binary function.

It is just good to have a helpful context of how those things fit into the overall process, because they are all interrelated. Everything has an intelligence, and what alchemists are learning to do is create an effective means of being able to integrate intelligences normally experienced as external, in a way that is philosophically sound. Methods taught within the Western Mysteries are safer than a lot of other teachings, and lead to the right kind of understanding. It is that understanding that is actually the most important part of the whole process.

The doing of things is a demonstration of understanding: The bottom line really is, the understanding that enables the doing.

XXI

Stones in the Work

The Stones in the work are different than the potables. Potable Gold and Potable Silver, the philosophical Sulphurs are obtained by putting elemental gold or silver in Philosophic Mercury. If one were to work toward creation of the Philosopher's Stone, the philosophical Sulphur of gold would be needed as a ferment for the red Stone at a specific point in the process.

Of course, the white Stone, which can be fermented with the philosophical Sulphur of silver is achievable before going through the entire process again to get to the red Stone. One should practice with the fermentation of the white Stone before moving on the the red Stone, because silver is less costly to work with until the process and proper ratios are perfected enough to move into working with gold.

Success with the white Stone has its own rewards though: The white Stone cures diseases of the mind, performs lunar related functions including the perfection of the Lunar body, and transmutes base metals into white noble metals such as silver, platinum, and uranium. The red Stone cures all physical illness, rejuvenates the physical body, performs solar related functions including perfection of the Solar body, and transmutes base metals into gold.

Metallic transmutation was not the goal of the true adepts. They would not pull two hairs for a pile of gold, for the most part, unless they had a reason like something they needed to do, and that was just part of the process. But truly, by the time adepts become masters, and can make the Elixir of Life from the Philosopher's Stone, they can transcend their bodies anytime they wish. They can go anywhere as truly spiritual sovereigns.

Masters do not need gold, but transmutation is still vital because that is the test for whether the Stone is real or not. If it does not transmute it is not the Universal Medicine. That is why transmutation was a vital part of the process and that is why it has become part of the story. That is the part that everybody knows even though they do not know why. So these things have tests as part of an inherent check and balance system, because if it is not a Stone it is probably poison. Testing of transmutation is vital: If it does not transmute, then it will probably prove fatal. Ingesting the improper dose of the real thing will kill one too, if not prepared for it. Elixir of Life doses must be taken in extreme dilution.

The stories of people having the Stone and dying is the direct result of what happens when people come upon things that they did not work to obtain, whether they died by foolishly ingesting things they did not understand, or through other means of foolishness.

Edward Kelly is a perfect case in point. He was a bit of a rogue, but he was a talented seer in Elizabethan times. He worked as a seer for John Dee, with whom he had a longstanding working relationship. John Dee was a very respectable man, considered the most educated man in the whole world. He is said to have had the largest personal library in the world, and worked as astrologer for Queen Elizabeth.

Dee's association with Edward Kelly caused him occasional trouble. Kelly was a bit of a scoundrel, but also a very talented seer, and since John Dee was not a very good seer, he had to rely on one.

At one point, Edward Kelly found a stash of transmutation powder, and of course in true roguery and ego, made transmutations for royal persons. He and Dee traveled throughout the courts of Europe, and got lodging and favors, and Kelly performed transmutations.

In the beginning, they did not know the power of the Stone they had, which turned out to be really, really powerful, because it had been multiplied many times. But they did not know that, so they wasted a whole bunch of it in transmutation without realizing they were using way too much of it. Again, due to their ignorance of not knowing to test it with a smaller portion first, they wasted a lot of it.

By the time they got done figuring that out, they did not have as big a portion of it left yet they still paraded around and made demonstrations. Instead of Edward Kelly saying, "I do not know how to make this but we found it and this proves that this is real," his ego could not just let him do that. He had to tell people that he was an alchemist and that he made it.

Well, when he ran out of it, that got him locked in a tower. What potentate would not want somebody that could just make gold for them?

John Dee eventually made his way back to England and was given a small pension. He lived out his life, not exactly in splendor, but not in squalor either. Edward Kelly ended up falling out of a tower window on his second attempt to escape from one or another of his little incarcerations, and broke his neck. That was the end of a perfectly good seer.

All of that could have been avoided, simply by telling the truth, like "Yeah, we found this powder. We found a stash of it and it really transmutes base metals. We'd like to do some research to figure it out." But, he always had the delusion that he could figure it out, even though he had been trying to figure it out for quite some time and not succeeded. I think he was truly delusional enough to believe that he was going to succeed.

Of course, if one did not do the work to get there originally, it is not going to happen. So, it is unfortunate, but these cases are documented. Those presentations in royal courts were recorded in front of people who had no reason to lie about it. Those courts had documenters that wrote down everything that happened and it is there in history, in black and white. So, there is no reason to doubt that those episodes happened.

It is just dumb to think about someone losing life for making grandiose claims of things that cannot be backed up because they are not true, when simply being honest would have avoided the entire problem.

That is another reason why it is a pet peeve of mine not to overstate one's level of accomplishment. For example, certain alchemical groups have courses that when passed, they send a little paper certificate that says 'Master Alchemist' or something equally ridiculous. I just about want to come out of my skin because I would never allow anyone to call me that. Until one can make the Philosopher's Stone, and has demonstrated the proof of it, one does not have the right to be called by the title of those adepts who have! That the 'alchemical' groups do not know any better is just as bad as the idea that somebody would parade around and think that they are a true Master Alchemist just because they got a certificate. At least one of the organizations does not even require any actual laboratory alchemy work if students are not comfortable with that process!

If that were not bad enough, those who have done that then go hold classes and teach Albertus plant alchemy *regurgita*, and students think they are learning alchemy.

Obviously, it bugs me. When I said something to an adept alchemist about that situation being annoying and about doing something about it, he said, "Why? The people that do all that do not want to learn real alchemy anyway. They just want to play with glassware and pretend they are doing alchemy." I was kind of irritated about that, but adepts have a certain viewpoint. I understand what he was saying and at the same time it is still irritating because there are people who really do want to learn real alchemy that would appreciate the truth. I know, I was one of them once upon a time.

The universe will bring seekers to the right place when they are ready, just as it always has for me. So, from one point of view, I agree. At the same time, not saying something when people are running around teaching nonproductive *regurgita*, the longer that is going to continue. At least informing those who are seeking the truth that there is an alternative path opens a dialogue for those that are ready to see the difference, rather than just deciding for them that they do not really want it.

The truth is that some people are starving for the truth. They have such a thirst for the truth that they are willing to drink sand and hope it will become water. Unfortunately for them, hoping does not make it so.

I feel the same way about much of what is being taught currently that is supposed to pass for actual magical instruction.

XXII

Mainstream Teaching vs. Adept Training in Alchemy & Magic

This is based on my experience, though I know it accords with the experience of many others who only continue their present courses because they have not yet been presented with viable alternatives.

Mainstream teaching is a lot of busy work: One learns the Hebrew letters, or studies charts and tables of symbols that are eventually supposed to be meaningful. Even Aleister Crowley made a joke about his Golden Dawn initiation, where he said they bound him to secrecy with terrible oaths and then confided to his safe keeping the Hebrew alphabet.[12]

With real adepts there is no busy work; there is just work. Furthermore, it is mostly 'doing' work that leads to practical understanding. They do not usually spell it all out, and they do not often connect all the dots. They give the work and see how the pupil does with it.

If pupils gain the understanding from the work they are supposed to get, then they get to go on to the next part. And if

---

[12] Fortune, Dion. "The Unwritten Qabalah." In The Mystical Qabalah, 27. London: E. Benn, 1957.

124

they do not, they do not. I do not know if they all do it that way, but that was my experience with most of them. The adept viewpoint is that 'practical' is what works, because what 'works' is real. However, it is not the same as 'doing something' because one believes it 'works' without the slightest care or understanding as to 'why.' I know many people who say, "I don't need to know why it works, as long as it works that is all I need to know." And, that is where they are stuck.

There is no, "I think this is real because I choose to believe it." That is not an adept viewpoint. If a pupil believes something, the adept is open minded enough to ask, "Why?" One better have a good reason other than just believing it because it is something that was taught to one before, and just accepted.

That is really what 'belief' is. There is a huge difference between believing and knowing. If one knows, one does not need to believe. One only believes when one does not know. Just believing is dangerous, and that is why adepts are very big on not making assumptions. So, it is okay to declare what is not known, but do not make assumptions about things. It is one of the hardest things for seekers to learn, or rather, unlearn.

That is where most modern magical training goes off track. It is kind of like the adolescent phase of growing up from a revivalist birth, which is still progress in evolution and growth, but currently more pomp than substance.

There are a number of independent thinking magical people that put unique content out, but there is still too much *regurgita* and not nearly enough actual thought about it, like planetary hours and a bunch of other stuff non-adepts made up and passed off as being of substance.

When one understands that the Sun and the Moon have nothing

to do with where the physical luminaries are, one can do the inner work and it does not matter, because they are all inside on a microcosmic level. If they are all inside, planetary hours are irrelevant.

I am not saying that celestial bodies do not have influence, clearly, the moon does. It has influence on us and living things and the earth itself. One would have to be an idiot to disagree with that. As to what the other planets do and what influences they may or may not have, that is not really the point.

Again, the point is, that those intelligences are nonphysical. Those forces are everywhere, they permeate every stitch in the fabric of creation, but they also have a physical representation on the level of the solar system within those planets that are their namesakes. Everything physical still has a nonphysical intelligence. That is all there is, physical and nonphysical. In the nonphysical, there are all kinds of compartments that exist, but still, they are nonphysical. Those nonphysical intelligences exist in their own right, but they also have physical anchors, and when the anchors move, the range of what they influence fluctuates. Psyches within their range of influence, that have not yet been liberated from the effects of those forces, are influenced to whatever degree each of them still holds sway within each individual's psyche.

From a magical point of view though, it is kind of irrelevant. It is like saying a car moves because it has gears. There is no need to focus on the gears to get in the car and drive it down the road.

We have the body. We have all the parts. We do not need to focus on what the planets are doing. We need to focus on what our own parts are doing, and learn how to make them do what we need to learn how to make them do. We do not have to worry about where Jupiter is.

It is really a distraction. Understanding 'why' is the key to spiritual evolution, not just acceptance. And the final word is, if one does not understand why, then one does not fully understand. And that is okay. Being aware that one does not fully understand is then what drives one to go seeking until one does.

There are places where I have blind spots and I am aware of them. There may be others that I am not aware of yet because I did not get around those corners, but I am aware of a few of them. And as I do research and continually strive towards understanding them, those pieces come. Learning to see the way through darkness is just part of the process. Often pieces come in surprising ways. In my case there is a set of seven things that I need to gain understanding around to do the next step in a particular process, and I have four of them. I had two of them two years ago, then another one year ago, and I got the fourth one the other day. How long it takes for the three others to come, I do not know. But it is important for a certain viewpoint of the particular process that is required for me to go on to one of the next things that I am supposed to understand.

In between all these things we are supposed to come to understand, there are also things we need to get done, so the Higher Genii throttle development to a degree, because we cannot get where we need to go before it is time to get there. We cannot ripen before we are ready to be ripe because we are not the only ones in the Garden, we are connected to everything else.

Having a purpose also means one cannot be ahead of schedule, or risk screwing up everybody else's training schedule. Personally, I am just glad I do not have to be in charge of that. All I have to do is my best: Make an effort, keep doing it, do not stop, ever.

That means every day it looks a little different. I have work to do, plus exercises and practices, in addition to all the lab work testing out different *Ens* processes and figuring out what it takes to make Melissa plants happy. Sometimes I water them and they look fine, and three hours later I walk by and they are all passed out, being dramatic.

The reason I teach on top of everything else is so that other seekers do not have to stumble around in the dark. We all stand on the shoulders of the people that came before us, and it is proper to honor them because they, too, were doing the best they could. Their Higher Genii were in control and those pieces needed to be put into place. That is just how the game works. So I am putting the pieces I have on the board.

That is why I love alchemy, because at least I know when playing the game that my pieces are validated because stuff works. It is not just belief. Even in magic where there are extreme experiences that are valid, if only because they are extreme experiences, there is not always the check and balance system to know whether those extreme experiences are what they are thought to be or not. It takes a certain level of consciousness to be developed to discern the difference, because those intelligences whose job it is to keep everyone in the box until they are ready to get out of the box are the most clever intelligences that exist in the entire universe, aside from God, the One Mind.

It is their job to keep the unevolved in that box. If they have to give delusions of grandeur to keep seekers trapped, they will. If one does not know that is what they are doing, or one is content to roll around in delusions, then there is no more evolution and they did their job. That is something that must be guarded against continually. Just because one has an experience does not make one king of the world, it just means some progress was made on an evolutionary path. Progress in alchemy and magic often comes in interesting and unexpected ways.

It was not too long after I started doing artwork again, drawing archetypal imagery, I was connecting to certain forces, which a long time ago I honestly always thought was a little bit airy fairy. I always had artistic ability, but for years I never really did anything with it because I was too busy dealing with business. I just repressed all that, and then it got to the point where I could not.

I had to draw these things, because the intelligences that were coming through wanted depiction. In the beginning I still resisted doing it, but it got to the point where they would not let me sleep. Depicting them gives them an anchored form, which they were insistent upon having, and provides a conduit if one's consciousness is ready to maintain the connection. When I started working on one that was an underworld Guardian over several days, I got taken out of my sleep, pulled through a veil, into a whole other level of reality in the underworld itself. That had never happened before. It is humbling to say the least.

So one of the magical things I find interesting is that for all the talk of evocation in the community, one of the things most magical practitioners do not seem to realize is, if one has the power to evoke a powerful entity into this world and a connection is made with it, it has the power to pull one back into its world too.

Nobody talks about that. Until it happens personally, one would not realize that it is actually true. And, thinking that drawing a little chalk circle on the floor, or drawing stars in the air, is going to stop that from happening is a sure sign that means one does not understand how evocation works.

129

There is much to cover on the magical side of things, but it is better to get a strong foundation on the alchemical side of things first, so that when discussing magical things, references to basic alchemical concepts have been explored enough to make sense in relation to magic.

Give the information in this book serious thought and consideration. Studying, not just reading, this text regularly will be repaid with the organized flow of its information into the psyche. The haphazard planting of seeds does not do the wisdom of the Western Mysteries justice. It is my sincere hope that the seeds planted herein will take root and grow within seekers to lay a path of truly productive spiritual work that accelerates personal evolution into an entirely new paradigm.

God speed to the Sons of Art.

About Aethyrius

Aethyrius is an instructor in the Western Mystery Tradition with over 25 years of unique experience, study, research, and practical work. He has had the honor of direct study under multiple true adepts on both sides of the Hermetic Arts: Practical Alchemy & Magic. Insights gained from such a privileged position give him unique and refreshing viewpoints on aspects of the Western Mysteries that make spiritual work both practical and accessible to seekers of the Mysteries.

He is the creator of the Transcendence Oracle™ and founder of Transcendence Works!

Aethyrius has private working groups and teaches Initiatory Seership, Practical Alchemy, and Deep Magic based upon his experience of true initiatory streams within the Western Mystery Tradition.

He can be contacted through his website:

https://www.transcendenceworks.com